A FLAG FOR THE MATABELE

A FLAG FOR THE MATABELE

An Entertainment in African History

by

PETER GIBBS

NEW YORK
THE VANGUARD PRESS

The Admiral pulled to the islands three;
The kings saluted him gracious*lee*.
The Admiral, pleased at his welcome warm,
Unrolled a printed Alliance form.

"Your Majesty, sign me this, I pray—
I come in a friendly kind of way—
I come, if you please, with the best intents,
And Queen Victoria's compliments."

From W. S. GILBERT'S
"The Three Kings of Chickeraboo"

I

In the gracious shadow of Government House, at Bulawayo, there stands a little round hut. Its conical thatched roof has a decided kink and the apex leans over to one side a little rakishly, like a clown's hat with too heavy a bobble. Its back is turned on the big house, not disdainfully, but in very proper perception of its own station, for it was once the pioneer of official residencies in Rhodesia, built without benefit of architects in the days before elegance came to the land.

The little hut was built of mud in the very best style of the day, and after fifty years of burning sun alternating with lashing rain it still stands as solid as ever. Its thick whitewashed walls certainly bulge a little drunkenly, and at the end of the dry season, when the grass round it is bleached white too, it looks more like a snow house rising out of the ground than something that has been built on the surface.

Viewing it from any distance one feels that, in a strong wind, the whole thing ought to crumple up sideways. As it has not done so during the fifty odd years since it was built there would appear no imminent danger. A closer view entirely contradicts the impression of frailty, for the snowlike wall is solid earth and the roof sparkling in the sunlight is a deep and abiding thatch.

It must have been a modest establishment as official residencies go. By modern standards it would serve as a comfortable bathroom, although there is no evidence that, even as a habitation, it ever boasted any plumbing. It stands about twenty feet in diameter and six feet high under the eaves. Inside, the roof is lined with an old whitewashed sailcloth for a ceiling, hanging down forlornly in the centre. The more intimate appointments have long since been removed—which, in view of the dearth of plumbing, is probably as well—but there still stands in the hut to-day a heavy horsehair couch, covered with a shiny chocolate patent leather from which, to use Ian Hay's inimitable expression, the patent has palpably expired. It is an aggressively masculine couch and bears witness to the lack of petticoat influence in the residency circles of the day, for it is far too unyielding to have been of much use even for the opening skirmishes of serious diplomacy. It is, in fact, a piece of furniture that would be scorned in any ambitious chancellory.

The only window in the hut faces south, which is a convenient aspect for a window in the tropics south of the equator. Whoever put it there showed a perception that has escaped many later-day architects. Of course, the builders of the hut may have put the window where they did because that was the direction in which they wanted to look out. To-day it looks on the discreet back of Government House and any real view is blotted out by tall trees which have been planted in the grounds. But when the little hut was built, and the thorn bush round it had been cleared away, the big man who often came to occupy it looked out across the land that fell away before him, over the veld in the direction of the Matopo hills rising somewhere beyond the horizon.

To-day, if you want to see the view, you must leave the hut and go forward past the trees. Then you too will see how the country falls away before you. But, instead of thorn bush and open pasture land, you will look out across a modern white man's city with blocks of flats and breweries belching smoke, and ungainly cooling towers of a power station standing high as hills themselves. To one side you will see the red roofs of white men's houses poking themselves inquisitively through deep green tree-tops—or, if it is October, through the blue haze of jacaranda blossom, bluer even than the sky. And to the other side, in regimented lines, flowing like a swelling sea over the even veld, waves of grey roofs under which dwell in their tens of thousands—and in careful separation from the white men—the grandchildren of those black people who once fled before the builders of the little hut into the shelter of the Matopos.

But that is a story we will come to later. First, let us get back to the hut, for there it still stands for us to visit to-day. The only window is in a little bay, built out like a porch, again presumably without any professional guidance in its design. There is a common sash-type window-frame which has miraculously stood the test of time. This window must surely boast an unenviable distinction, for it was probably the very one that introduced to the primitive African interior the doubtful boon of breakable sash cords and weights whose inherent feature was to fall out of reach. Thus to the Dark Continent came one of the first blessings of civilization.

At the west point of the hut—there are no sides in a round building, and we must be precise—there is a plain deal door with the inevitable loose brass door-knob which has presumably been on the point of falling off for forty-nine years. The door opens through a second little porch formed by two mud buttresses, each rising from a heap of whitewashed stones. It was through this door that the big men of the eighteen-nineties in Africa—the empire builders—passed, and they had to be careful not to bump their heads.

Cecil Rhodes occupied the hut on his visits to Bulawayo in Rhodesia's early days. It was built, not inappropriately, on the ground where the Matabele king, Lobengula, from whom Rhodes took the land, had held court before him. Lobengula called the seat of government his kraal, which also means a stable, but from the wider choice of our own language we can offer the refinement and call it a camp, although his own word was, perhaps unintentionally, more apposite.

When the white men ultimately came to the land in force—and that, too, is a story we will come to—Lobengula's camp was burnt down and the little hut rose in its place.

By all standards, Lobengula's residency had been a far more ambitious establishment than Rhodes hut. It was a big camp, roughly circular, and about half a mile in diameter. Round the outer rim of the circle, in regular stockaded segments, lived the King's household troops and attendants. If any intruders had wanted to get at the King and do him violence—such as he well deserved at the avenging hands of many neighbouring tribes—they would have had to fight their way through a phalanx of guards, whichever way they attacked. In this outer ring of the circle there were a couple of hundred huts. If the modern African's inherited delight in cramped, airless quarters, shared with countless of his fellows, is anything to go by, the King's personal guard must have run to considerable proportions.

In the centre of the camp, inside an inner stockaded ring, and tastefully set within aromatic range of the goat kraal, the King had his own spacious house. An equally spacious building alongside quite properly accommodated his wagon. His queens—and he had several—and their attendants occupied a less prominent, but fashionably overcrowded, part of the central camp. In actual fact, the queens could not complain that they were treated any less favourably than the goats or the sacred black cattle and that, in Matabele eyes, was quite a concession. The rubbish heap, an indispensable part of the royal enclosure, was thoughtfully sited down wind.

There were hardly more than a dozen trees left dotted about the camp and, because Matabeleland was not a democracy, but a land of privileged classes, the royal goats were given the shadiest of these in their kraal. This tree still grows there to-day, somewhat dwarfed by the statelier trees planted by our intrusive civilization. A hundred yards or so from the little hut, it stands preserved as a national monument, for it was under this tree, in company with the goats and their ever-attendant flies, that Lobengula, King of the Matabele, held his court and here the first chapters of the recorded history of Rhodesia were written.

Like all the indigenous trees of Matabeleland with their sparse leaves, it offers poor shade under the tropic sun, but Lobengula and the goats no doubt enjoyed rubbing their backs against it. Its gnarled roots break the surface of the ground all round the two main trunks, which in their turn spread to more trunks curled and intertwined like the arms of an octopus. Just high enough for a tall man to stand under, the branches spread to a circle of thirty feet or so and round part of the circle they drop to the ground like a curtain. Neatly kept to-day, the tree suggests comfortable chairs and tea-parties under its shade. When it held pride of place in Lobengula's time, the guests sat inside the kraal on a carpet of goats' dung, and refreshments consisted of kaffir beer considerably less matured than the meat which accompanied it. The sacred black cattle were kept in an adjoining kraal on the other side of the stockade, and between the kraals the flies commuted—as the Americans say—with an unremitting sense of duty.

At one time, towards the close of the nineteenth century, this goat kraal was the focal point of interest in Africa among those who moved in the splendid world of courts and chancellories in Europe. Even the Queen of England, who had decided views on the proprieties, sent a mission of guardsmen to pay her respects to the portly savage who sat under the indaba tree in an advanced state of undress. For there was a time when Lobengula—who was repulsively fat and dressed himself unassumingly in a kilt of monkey-skin of the briefest Bikini cut—was the most courted monarch in the world. Somehow or other he had acquired a British Navy cap whose style he improved with an application of ostrich feathers and his visitors, averting their gaze from the unwholesome void between the cap and the kilt, said he looked every inch a king.

Not that he set any great store on the blandishments and flattery that were showered on him. It did not take him long to form his own opinion of these peculiarly dressed and anæmic-complexioned people who came and squatted uncomfortably on the goats' dung in front of him. He told them quite frankly that all white men were liars and only came to see him when they wanted to get something.

Although the first assertion may have been prejudiced by the behaviour of some of his visitors, the second was perfectly right.

II

THE Matabele throne under the indaba tree was hardly the seat of a long-established dynasty. Lobengula had the barren distinction of being the only Matabele king to accede to the throne in his own country. Less than forty years before, the fathers of his subjects had still been part of the mighty Zulu people whose lands were a thousand miles to the south. His own father, M'Zilikazi, had broken with the Zulus and led his tribe north across the Limpopo, and the Matabele became a nation with as envied a reputation for savagery as the great Zulus themselves.

As arises in the chronicled histories of even the more enlightened nations—depending on whether they were written by those who had suffered or gained from the events —there was a difference of opinion about the true reason for M'Zilikazi's defection from the Zulus. Some said that although he was one of the subservient chiefs to Shaka, the great King of the Zulus, the opportunities presented by his military duties were too much of a temptation and he indulged on the side in plunder and pillage on his own account. In consequence, he had to fly north to escape the savage, if understandable, wrath of his king, for in those days plunder was the acknowledged prerogative of the state, without any of the modern ideological pretensions to disguise it. The other theory, held not unnaturally by the Matabele people themselves, was that M'Zilikazi was a chief in his own right but that Shaka had conquered and suppressed him. M'Zilikazi, they said, pretended to submit and ostentatiously built a city for his tribe near Eshowe, in Zululand, which is now Natal. There he is said to have gathered round him what were to become the Matabele people and, when he felt strong and independent enough, to have deserted Shaka and led his nation northwards to find hunting grounds of their own.

Whichever may have been the truth, there is no doubt that M'Zilikazi did build a city for the Matabele before he left Zululand, and he called it Bulawayo, "the place of slaughter". When at last he came to the high lands between the Limpopo and the Zambesi, and settled his people in their new country, he built another city and called it Bulawayo too, although it is unlikely that he did so on a sentimental impulse. It is often said that the present Bulawayo came to be so called because M'Zilikazi exercised his robust methods of discipline over his people to some purpose there. It seems more likely, in the light of history, that he himself perpetuated the name and memories of the old Bulawayo, lest there should become established in the minds of his subjects any unwarranted hope that, in the new city, discipline was to be relaxed.

M'Zilikazi led his tribe away from the Zulus at the time when the Dutch settlers in the Cape Colony—at the southern tip of the African continent—were starting to turn their faces northwards too. At the beginning of the nineteenth century the Boers had moved east from Cape Town and were linking up with the British settlers who had established a beach-head on the continent farther up the coast round Algoa Bay, where Port Elizabeth now stands. The process, until then, had not been so much a movement as an infiltration. But all the time there was building up against the settlers, spreading themselves along the fair littoral of the Cape, a mounting resistance of kaffir tribes, from the Zulus, the Pondos, the Tembus and the Xosas. And the most irritating—because they were the most effective—were the Zulus under Shaka.

The Boers were determined to shake themselves free of this kaffir menace and to establish their own white civilization in the empty plains of the north. From this urge was born the goal of a land of exclusive white settlement that still survives as their political faith to-day. They maintain, quite reasonably, that when they moved north into what were to become the Orange Free State and the Transvaal Republic they sought to evade the natives, not to displace them. Some of them, however, under Piet Retief, did turn aside from this amiable purpose when, from the bleak heights of the Drakensberg mountains, they saw the inviting valleys of Natal sweeping down like lovely gardens to the sea. Zulus or no Zulus, this looked to them like the Promised Land and, being faithful adherents to the teachings of the Bible, they saw no reason why it should not be theirs.

Shaka was dead. During his lifetime he had caused to be murdered at least a million people, which was no small achievement considering he had none of the scientific aids enjoyed by the later masters of human massacre. His brother Dingaan who, incidentally, had killed him, reigned in his stead. Dingaan combined his brother's savagery with a useful touch of guile. With protestations of welcome, he signed a treaty ceding territory to the Boers and, at a subsequent feasting, to which Retief and sixty-eight men had, on implicit invitation, come unarmed, he signalled his Zulu warriors and they up and butchered the lot. Then they went out and massacred the wives and children who were waiting for their men to return from the party.

That was on the sixth of February 1838. Less than twelve months later, on the sixteenth of December in the same year, Andries Pretorius, the new Boer Commandant-General, avenged Retief at Blood River when Dingaan was routed and his Zulu regiments were decimated. To-day the Union of South Africa celebrates the sixteenth of December as a national holiday. For years it was called

Dingaan's Day and, although the name perpetuated an
evil memory, at least everybody knew why. But, in a land
where the native is held in little honour, prominence for
a black man's name, in any context, is thought inexpedient,
so now it is called the Day of the Covenant—a name which
should effectively obscure its origin. As years go on the
story of Blood River, like so many old stories, will be forgotten and the name Dingaan will merely signify the rather
unaccountable title of a horse race.

As a date, the sixth of February will be forgotten too—it
is already. But on that morning, more than a hundred
years ago, there was planted in the heart of the Boer a loath-
ing for black men that has passed down as an inheritance
for three and more generations, and has so far never been
erased.

These things happened a thousand miles or more from
the plain on the high veld where the new Bulawayo was
one day to stand. But from them followed the whole course
of events that are now recorded as the early history of
Rhodesia.

Although Southern Africa is an arid country, much
addicted to long periods of drought, four rivers have played
a dominant part in her history. Two of them flow west-
ward into the Atlantic, and two east into the Indian Ocean.
These four rivers are different from the usual run of African
rivers south of the equator. It is a hackneyed joke that a
man falling into a South African river runs the risk of
suffocation by dust. There is a river in the Transvaal called
the Sand River, and for three-quarters of the year it could
not bear a more appropriate name. In the rainy season,
these rivers come down tempestuously in flood—and
incidentally bring a fair measure of the topsoil of the
country with them, so that next dry season it is more arid
still—but when the floods have passed they remain but
strings of stagnant pools, left to evaporate in the heat of the
burning sun or seep down into the thirsty earth below.

But there are four rivers that are mighty rivers and at each new advance of the white man northward into the interior of Africa one of them has held him at bay. For they are rivers that still flow strongly, months after the rains have stopped, through deep gorges and over thundering rapids. In flood, they are impassable—or, at least, they were in the days before high bridges were built over them. The bridges that connect Africa's life lines to-day—her roads and railways—over the Orange, the Vaal, the Limpopo and the Zambesi, are probably her most vulnerable strategic points. For the rivers are not like the rivers of Europe where armies can come along and replace blown bridges with improvised crossings overnight. The bridges over the Orange at Hopetown, and the Zambesi at the Victoria Falls, tower hundreds of feet above the river beds. Below them is no smooth reach of placid water, with nothing worse than the strength of the current to hamper a crossing—but monster rocks and tortuous gullies and inhospitable rapids. The cliffs of the gorges fall sheer, and only high above the level of the rivers has man been able to make his journeyings across them independent of the seasons.

The first river that stopped the white men was the Orange. It rises in the heights of the Drakensberg, almost within sight of the Indian Ocean. In the winter, snow falls heavily on the Drakensberg mountains, and much of the waters that wind their boisterous way thirteen hundred miles across to the farther side of the parched continent—through the burning plains of South West Africa out into the Atlantic—first came down to earth in little frozen flakes. The Boers saw the Orange River early in the eighteenth century, but they did not cross it for a hundred years. When they did, and on its northern bank proclaimed the Orange Free State—its freedom inherent in its river boundary—they were held back from moving farther northward by the Vaal.

The Vaal is but a tributary of the Orange, but there is nothing obsequious about it. In later days it has borne giant flying-boats on the bosom of its dam—until jet travel has made flying boats as outmoded as Boer wagons. It too rises in the Drakensberg, much farther north, and flows down in a majestic sweep to west and south. In their time the Boers crossed the Vaal as well, and the name of their new country, the Transvaal, proclaimed another obstacle surmounted. After that, all that stopped them going farther north was what Kipling called the " great grey-green, greasy Limpopo " which is more alliterative than strictly accurate.

In the great migration north during the nineteenth century it was M'Zilikazi who crossed the Limpopo first. In 1835, about three years before Dingaan was routed, M'Zilikazi led his warriors, in unbecoming flight, into the sanctuary of the empty country to the north. He had left Zululand and its unpalatable memories of Shaka behind him, and had set off with the notion of crossing the Vaal and settling his people on the rich high veld. The same idea had also occurred to the Boers at the same time. They had come many hundreds of miles expressly to get away from the kaffirs. In fact, they had come so far and their journey had seemed so long that their sense of geographic proportion had become confused and in one stream in the heart of what was to be the Transvaal—still thousands of miles south of the equator—they thought they had reached the source of the Nile, and so they called it Nylstrom, and a considerable town boasts that inappropriate name to-day. It was a still more disappointing reality when they found they had not even shaken off their unsociable neighbours from the coast.

But the Matabele were in front now, on the move, and the Boers were determined to keep them moving. As they worked their way across the innocent looking plains—where, under the waving grass, lay, blessedly unsuspected, the richest goldfields in the world—they chased the kaffirs before them. Paul Kruger, as a boy, learnt to fight in this war. Sixty years later he used the knowledge he thus gained to fight the English whom he grew to hate as much as the kaffirs. It was in the Marico, where the lovely orange groves of Zeerust blossom to-day, that M'Zilikazi was finally put to flight.

He and his people climbed laboriously up on to the empty plateau still farther north, into the country between the two great rivers that flow into the Indian Ocean—the Limpopo and the Zambesi—the country which came to be called Matabeleland. This was the land of which even the Zulus knew little. It was virtually unknown to the white men. On their maps they marked it "the Kingdom of Monomopata "—mythical, Gilbertian.

Here, on the high plains, M'Zilikazi settled his people and founded a new kingdom. The Matabele were at last established as a nation in their new land. M'Zilikazi built his new city with the old name of Bulawayo, from whence his people spread out across the country. Not more than fifty-five years later, a little Scots doctor named Jameson, with a band of adventurers as diminutive as himself, followed M'Zilikazi into the country between the Limpopo and the Zambesi and placed his own Queen's flag at the site of another new city with the old name of Salisbury. From Salisbury the white people spread out across the land, and the two circles whose centres were Bulawayo and Salisbury, three hundred miles apart, overlapped and inevitably clashed.

M'Zilikazi had certainly got there first. The way he brought a primitive people out of bondage, to a land of promise a thousand miles away, stands for all time as an epic of leadership and faith. Yet it is not unprofitable to bear in mind the true course of events when the early white settlers in what was to become Rhodesia are incontinently accused of dispossessing the Matabele of their traditional home.

As soon as M'Zilikazi had settled his people in their new land his old habits reasserted themselves and he cast round in search of convenient neighbours to plunder. There was ample scope for his talents among the lesser tribes long established in these parts, such as the Mashonas and the Makalangas. He made a practice of leading these profitable raids himself. Once, when he was thus engaged, the rumour—born probably of wishful thinking—spread in Bulawayo that he was killed, and inevitable intrigue for the succession ensued among his people. Inconveniently, the King marched back at the height of the dispute, and the barbaric purge of those who had misguidedly proposed to set a new king in the place of one they genuinely believed to be dead has only been rivalled by the dictators of the more civilized world.

There is historical doubt whether the King's first son, who not unreasonably had been nominated for the throne, was executed. In any case, he could not be found when the King did eventually die. The second son, Lobengula, wisely withdrew into the comparative safety of the spirit-ridden Matopo hills, although death at the hand of his father would have been more in the tradition of his race than his ultimate wretched fate.

M'Zilikazi died in 1868, leaving a pardonable doubt among the people as to who was to be his successor. The old tyrant's purges were not easily forgotten and any claimant for the throne might have been excused for looking a little nervously over his shoulder. His people buried the dead King as he had wished, in the heart of the Matopo hills, among the tumbled granite boulders. They sat him upright in a cave, facing north, the way he had brought them out of bondage. Later, Rhodes was to say of him, "What a poet the man was! ", and to follow his lyrical example.

Not until the old man's remains had been safely walled in—and his wagons had also been interred in an adjacent cave, handy for use in his new sphere—did the witch doctors venture forth with Lobengula, their candidate for the throne. That was nearly two years later, in 1870. When Lobengula entered on his reign over a horde of primitive savages who had never seen a written word, the second Reform Bill was already law in England, putting two million new voters on the roll; Cecil Rhodes, delicate son of a Norfolk clergyman, had just landed in South Africa for his health; and Leander Starr Jameson had entered a medical school in London.

But in Bulawayo, the new King sat under the indaba tree, sunning his expanding paunch. He and his people had never heard of that other world, although in twenty-three short years it was to intrude, even into his malodorous kraal, and to burn it down, and drive him off, and set up its own strange civilization in "the place of slaughter".

III

WHEN Lobengula entered into his unenviable kingship, the way of the life of the Matabele people,
like the way of life of their ancestors, was based on
the simple and satisfactory principle of survival of the physi-
cally fittest. There was no nonsense about the rights of
the under-privileged, nor about unnatural doctrines that
preached equal opportunities for all. Ideas like these would
only have brought confusion and unhappiness to the
people.

Then, to shatter this African idyll, came the missionaries.
Men like Livingstone, Moffat, Carnegie, Helm—sincerity
their strength and their armour—left civilization and safety
thousands of miles behind and, pushing forward into uncharted lands where wild beasts and wild men competed for
the privilege of having them for breakfast, laboured thank-
lessly to preach their gospel of Christianity. Their work
was wholly altruistic. On Dr. Livingstone's memorial in
Westminster Abbey is inscribed, "For thirty years his life
was spent in an unwearied effort to evangelize the native
races, to explore the undiscovered secrets."

They were more successful in discovery than in evan-
gelization. In twenty-eight years of selfless toil, the faithful
workers of the Matabele mission scored two baptized con-
verts and, for all his piety and singleness of purpose, Dr.
Livingstone has gone down in history among the people of
Africa, not so much as a divine, but as the first white man
to see the Victoria Falls.

In the missionaries' wake followed the traders and it was

they who dispensed the true comforts. Like the missionaries, these strange men with light skins bore themselves with an air of superiority and, moving singly and unafraid among hordes of potential assassins, established a respect for their persons which others were unable to uphold when they came in armed force.

But it was a German scientist and explorer, Karl Mauch, who first found in the land an attraction for the white man that depended neither on converting nor compounding with the natives. He discovered gold in Mashonaland—or what had been left of it by the ancients. For many believed, and many still do to-day, that this was where King Solomon and the Queen of Sheba had dug out their contemporary fortunes.

Mauch reported that the extent and beauty of the goldfields were such that, when he saw them, he " stood transfixed ", unable to use his hammer, as if the Mashonaland horizons stretched into limitless distances with bright nuggets lying all over the place enhancing the scenic beauty. His eulogy tended to disregard the fact that gold-bearing rock usually lies hundreds of feet underground and that Mashonaland scenery is, on the whole, comparatively uninteresting.

However, Mauch exhibited specimens of quartz to the Royal Geographic Society in London and engendered a far wider interest in the country than the London Missionary Society could ever have hoped to achieve. Fabulous stories were spread of the wealth of Monomopata, and the true adventurers of the civilized world set out to win, not the gold, but Lobengula's exclusive permission to dig for it, which would be worth considerably more.

For it was Lobengula and his Matabele who were the main obstacles in the path of the fortune seekers. Although the gold between the Limpopo and the Zambesi was first found in Mashonaland, outside the actual territory that Lobengula's people might be expected to claim as their own, the Matabele dominated the whole country and it would have been foolhardy to a degree to have started digging for treasure without the King's enthusiastic consent.

So, to Lobengula's unprepossessing court at Bulawayo came Portuguese, Germans, Dutchmen and Britishers, and they grovelled at his leathery black feet, importuning him for a concession of the right to dig. Not one of them, if he found himself the lucky recipient, had any intention of using that right. He would be off back to civilization as fast as his lumbering wagon could carry him, to sell to the highest bidder.

The King's constitutional function was, by tradition, to lead his impis on raids for cattle and women from the neighbouring tribes with the laudable object of increasing his population both animal and human. Now he found his time almost wholly engaged in that technique of diplomatic argument with which the white man cloaks his own equally acquisitive intentions. He found he had to learn a new form of warfare, but as long as it was waged with only the spoken word he was quite able to hold his own. He said, "There is a wall built round the word of a chief," and implied he would hold the words of others just as inviolable. It was when the white men brought out their mysterious weapon of pen and paper that he was outmanœuvred, for he believed they meant what they wrote.

His first essay in treaty-making had been with John Moffat, son of the old pioneer missionary. John had once been a missionary in Matabeleland himself, but apparently the lack of results had discouraged him. Perhaps he felt that the natives could be more profitably converted from their barbarism by a nation than by a church. In any case, he had forsaken his spiritual allegiance, and now he was back in Bulawayo in the service of his temporal Queen. There, on her behalf, he persuaded Lobengula to sign with a cross—the illiterate mark that one day was to be worth a million pounds to someone else—acknowledgment of a treaty which undertook, in the first breath, " that peace and amity shall continue for ever between Her Britannic Majesty, Her subjects, and the Matabele people". The Matabele War with Britain, that wiped out Lobengula and many of his people, came five years later.

This solemn treaty, between the Widow of Windsor and the polygamist of Bulawayo, went on to record Lobengula's undertaking not to enter into any correspondence or treaty with any other state—such as any of Her Britannic Majesty's closer neighbours who might be so shameless as to have covetous eyes on his country—and not to sell his land to anybody. Beyond the promise of eternal peace, for what it proved to be worth, Lobengula got nothing in return for his undertaking, and the land was preserved for the Queen's subjects subsequently to take themselves.

Among the applicants at Lobengula's fly-infested kraal for his permission to dig for gold were three representatives of South Africa's newly-risen financial colossus, Cecil Rhodes. They were contemporaries of his from that incongruous world six thousand miles away whence he came. One, Charles Rudd, who had been a partner of Rhodes on the diamond diggings at Kimberley, was an old Harrovian and a Cambridge man, and the second, Rochfort Maguire, was a Fellow of All Souls. The third was Frank Thompson, a mere South African, one time secretary of Rhodes, who had some experience of natives and acted as interpreter.

Hour after hour, week after week and month after month, the unlettered King sat under the indaba tree arguing, with remarkable success, with the Cambridge graduate and the Oxford don. He tore to shreds their thesis on the advantage of granting Rhodes the concession. The pillars of learning, in fact, made so little headway that Rhodes felt constrained to force the issue. Being the richest man in South Africa he wielded a useful measure of influence in government, and even ecclesiastic, circles and he arranged for the deputy Commissioner of Bechuanaland, Sir Sidney Shippard—accompanied by none less than the Bishop of Bloemfontein—to make the uncomfortable journey to Bulawayo, to pay a timely courtesy visit to Lobengula. The Bishop's presence in the party divested the deputation of any suspicion of an ulterior motive, at least in the eyes of the watching world. Nor was its significance lost on Lobengula.

At the kraal, Sir Sidney rose gallantly to the demands of the occasion. He advanced to meet the King across the carpet of goats' dung, a splendid figure in frock coat and sun helmet, the helmet a little battered from the journey. On his breast flashed the cross of St. Michael and St. George, a shining magnet for the flies. He was an Oxford man too and, catching sight of Maguire, his surprise at meeting an old colleague in the middle of Africa was as studied as it was affecting. With a metaphorical wink in Rudd's direction, he blandly assured the King that Her Majesty's Government held no brief for private concession seekers and advised him, with a touching show of sincerity, to consider only the interests of his own people.

The frock coat and the glittering cross made a promising impression on Lobengula. The King's reaction to the Bishop was not, at first, altogether so fortunate. When the Bishop, feeling he ought to justify his inclusion in the deputation, tactlessly suggested the need to establish a mission school in Bulawayo, the King said, "I am the proper person to say if teachers are wanted"—a reply that led the Bishop later to complain that "some of Lobengula's arguments are quaint".

But any real dissension was happily averted, and Lobengula was, in due course, suitably impressed with the temporal and spiritual standing of his visitors. He remarked, too, that Her Britannic Majesty was apparently the only crowned head in Europe appreciative enough of his rank to send worthy visitors—a pronouncement that caused the Germans and Dutchmen hanging round the kraal to discount the English reputation for sportsmanship.

When the deputation withdrew it was in an aura of mutual goodwill and all the dignity an ox-wagon would permit, as it bumped its way back over the long dusty trail to the south. It says something for Sir Sidney's diplomacy —and much, too, for the Bishop's reticence—that Lobengula was so impressed with the inoffensive intentions of the British Government that he granted Rhodes' men a concession within a week. Pocketing it unceremoniously, Rudd and Maguire hurried south until they caught up with Sir Sidney and the Bishop, to whom they showed it with pride and well deserved thanks. The unfortunate Thompson was left behind in Bulawayo as a reminder to the King that he had entered into certain obligations, even though he might not be too sure what they were or what they implied.

The actual paper on which Lobengula placed his cross, and which came to be known as the Rudd Concession, was a breathless document. Its text was at least five hundred words—all in one sentence. In short, it set out that Rhodes' representatives would pay Lobengula—" King of Matabeleland, Mashonaland, and other adjoining territories "—a hundred pounds a month, and would make him a present of a thousand rifles and a hundred thousand ball cartridges, and a steamboat on the Zambesi "with guns suitable for defensive purposes ", and Lobengula in return would give to the said representatives, and their sons and their grandsons, all the metals and minerals in his " kingdoms, principalities and dominions ", and they could do anything with them they liked, and could "enjoy the profits—if any ", and because Lobengula had been "molested of late by divers persons " Rhodes' men could throw out of Lobengula's kingdom all trespassers and he would give them any help they needed and, what was more, would promise not to give the same things to anyone else unless the instalments were three months overdue.

The "kingdoms, principalities and dominions" were, of necessity, undefined, just as it was never disclosed by what authority, other than neighbourly terrorism, Lobengula claimed the kingship of Mashonaland. The Mashonas had dwelt in their country for many generations and, although they had never held allegiance to one paramount chief, they were a distinct tribe of their own, with their own local chiefs, and a far longer history of identity than the Matabele. However, the reference was flattering to Lobengula and went a long way to persuading him finally to sign. It was even more valuable in London, because Mashonaland was where the gold was. In fact, the kingship was no more incongruous than the gunboat on the Zambesi, which river, where it borders Matabeleland, is almost unnavigable anyway. But the vision of defensive guns trained against cowering Mashonas, in their kraals miles away from the river banks, must have given Lobengula some happy prospects.

Naturally, immediately after he had signed it, Lobengula denied he had ever assented to what was written into the Concession. His repudiation was enthusiastically encouraged by the less fortunate concession seekers who had been left empty-handed at his kraal. One and all they denounced the bad faith of these men who had prevailed on him to sign away those inalienable rights for which they had been importuning him themselves for months. The wretched Frank Thompson, a timid soul at the best of times, found it increasingly necessary to shun the limelight.

One of the unlucky ones went so far as to take with him all the way to England two of Lobengula's councillors—known as indunas—that they might protest to the great white Queen in person. The half-clad savages were received demonstratively by the British public, which is always enthusiastic about coloured races with whom it does not have to live in perpetual contact.

But, even in Britain, Rhodes had influence, and their programme of sight-seeing was carefully arranged lest they should go back to the depths of Africa with any wrong impressions. The highlight of their excursions was a visit to the army manœuvres at Aldershot where the object lesson of military strength such as the Matabele, even with a thousand rifles, could not hope to match, was not lost upon them. A visit to the Bank of England was, perhaps, a psychological mistake. They were shown the Queen's great horde of gold and, being simple men, uninhibited by the follies of civilization, they asked, if she had all this, why on earth should she want to send her people all the dreary way to Matabeleland for more?

They saw the Queen herself and talked to her through their interpreter. They were suitably impressed with her nobility and graciousness. But the way she covered the more feminine aspects of her person, in a manner their own women would have denounced as unnecessary, so disturbed them that they made poor work of the protests they had come so many thousands of miles to lodge. The whole visit was, in fact, so shrewdly stage-managed that when, on their return, they were given a permanent representative of the Queen in Bulawayo, in place of reversion of those rights which they had lost, neither of them recognized that another blow had been struck at the age-old independence of their people.

They came back to Lobengula full of the wonderful things they had seen; and, hearing what had been arranged, he could hardly be blamed for doubting if the journey had really been worth while. To compensate for his disappointment, he executed one of his indunas who had been enthusiastic about the Concession, and on whose advice he had been finally persuaded to sign. He put him to death with his whole family and pitched the bodies over the side of the hill, Thabas Induna, that stands in isolated relief, like a lone island in an empty sea, in the flat country north of Bulawayo. He fired the dead man's kraal and every living thing in it—men, women and children, horses, oxen and goats—so that they were all roasted alive. It was, if truth be known, but one of his minor purges, accounting only for sixty humans. But, on Frank Thompson, who witnessed the whole boisterous affair, it made a disquieting impression.

Thompson was now the sole representative in Bulawayo of a patently unpopular faction. He had had the comfortless experience, in his early youth, of seeing his own father murdered by natives. They had used the ingenious method of forcing a ramrod down his father's throat and the memory did little to bolster Frank's self-confidence. The shock, one morning shortly after the activities on Thabas Induna, of looking round and finding three black warriors with assegais close behind him, was too much. He jumped for the nearest point of vantage, which was a bare-backed horse, and galloped away from " the place of slaughter " and there was nothing furtive about his flight.

IV

I T was Frank Thompson's defection from his post in Bulawayo that was the direct cause of Dr. Jameson's entry into the ranks of those whose names in African history have become imperishable. Christened "Leander Starr", Jameson was destined for immortality anyway, for it is inconceivable that a man blessed with such epic names could be held to mediocrity—or even merely the sedate, if illustrious, prizes of the medical profession.

In Kimberley, in the diamond boom, he was bound in time to cross Rhodes' path and that, in itself, might have been enough to settle his fate. But it was Frank Thompson's fearful flight from Bulawayo that set him on the adventurous road of empire-building when, but the day before, such ambitions had not even crossed his mind.

Jameson had come to Kimberley about ten years before, in 1878. He was twenty-five then, born in the same year as Rhodes. He had been Resident Medical Officer in University College Hospital, in London—a signal honour for his age—and it is said that there he treated men and women with "masterly and humorous benevolence", the guiding propensity of his life. But, constitutionally, he was a wanderer. He had started off to see the world by the unconventional course of taking an opium addict on a voyage to America and back, and administering on the high seas a cure for the man's unfortunate habit. It was an experience which must have been of considerable value later, when called on to counter the effects of witch-doctors' treatment and to relieve Lobengula of gout.

Answering an advertisement in a London journal, Jameson took up a partnership in the diamond-boom town of Kimberley—marooned in the depths of dusty African veld —without any idea of what sort of place he was going to, but with the creditable intention of making enough money subsequently to indulge in a course of medical study in Vienna. In any event, he arrived ultimately at the court of Lobengula, whose atmosphere was in appreciable contrast to Viennese culture. Nor was Kimberley a potential stepping-stone in medical advancement. Like every other activity in the town, the practice of medicine had perforce to be rough and ready. Refinements in technique were neither available nor encouraged.

The partnership was short-lived because the senior, Dr. Prince, suffered an unfortunate attempt at blackmail by one of his lady patients who turned out to be less of a lady than he had imagined. Although Dr. Prince was vindicated at law, he retired and left the practice to Jameson. Jameson soon became the first doctor in Kimberley. His fame spread across the veld, and he was even called in by old President Brand of the Orange Free State, in Bloemfontein, whose Bright's disease was flourishing under a diet of tortoise soup, prescribed by a local missionary, the tortoises being caught in the town's muddy river.

Jameson achieved his greatest local notoriety when an epidemic of smallpox cropped up spasmodically—as it does even to-day—in various centres in South Africa. The diamond kings of Kimberley decided there could be no outbreak there, for it would be as fatal to business as to the unfortunate people who caught it. Labour and supplies were constantly needed from all parts of the continent and, if smallpox occurred in Kimberley, people would be discouraged from coming there, not, perhaps, so much through fear of catching the disease as through dread of the process of compulsory disinfection to which all newcomers to an infected area were summarily subjected.

Disinfection was not a pleasant process. For three long minutes the victim was incarcerated in a cramped sealed shed in which sulphur was burned, and if the fumes had little effect on any germs they were all but fatal to the patient. In the more enlightened centres, white men were allowed to stick their heads out through a hole in the wall of the shed, but this convenience was denied the natives, not on account of any misguided colour prejudice, but because their woolly hair was suspected of being a more likely lurking place for germs.

When some of the natives in Kimberley at last went down with suspicious symptoms—some of them dying, which was more significant still—the medical faculty of the town divided into two camps, those who pronounced the disease smallpox and those who emphatically did not. Jameson, who was a loyal friend of Rhodes, had no difficulty in attaching himself to the latter group; in fact he became its inspired leader. He came out with a comforting diagnosis of the scourge, calling it "a bulbous disease of the skin allied to pemphigus". As pemphigus is a rare medical condition, neither contagious nor fatal, the alarming spread and deadly effect of a disease merely allied to it was surprising.

The local Medical Officer of Health, Dr. Sauer—whom, only a short time before, Jameson had estranged by virtually stripping naked at poker—led the opposing camp. In the conflict that followed, when the two doctors themselves spoke their minds without any reticence whatsoever, and the general public openly and enthusiastically debated their respective degrees of professional integrity, they each brought libel actions against the other. Both won their respective suits, and the Court, nicely balancing the scales of justice, awarded the same damages in each case. The dispute was left, therefore, in the air, and any attempt to dogmatize on the true nature of the disease in Kimberley might, even to-day, constitute a contempt of court.

The friendship between Jameson and Cecil Rhodes that was to become ever closer and was to last throughout Rhodes' life, had started some years before when another young friend of Rhodes had been taken ill. It was to this friend, Neville Pickering, that Rhodes, in one of his early wills, bequeathed his fortune in trust, to be used "for the extension of the British Empire". An earlier will of Rhodes, made when he was only nineteen, when a fortune of any significance was still part of an adolescent dream, had graciously named the Secretary of State for the Colonies as trustee. A little later, perhaps because the person of the Secretary of State was too unpredictable, he added the name of Sidney Godolphin Alexander Shippard—he who was later to grace Lobengula's kraal with his frock coat.

When Rhodes' friendship with young Pickering grew, by which time the dream of fortune had in a few short years become reality, Shippard and the Secretary of State were summarily discarded and Rhodes made another will, much simpler in its terms. Without any frills, it stated, "I, C. J. Rhodes, being of sound mind, leave my worldly wealth to N. E. Pickering." Pickering was younger than Rhodes, and Rhodes lived his life in expectation of an early death.

But Neville Pickering was the first to go. He had been secretary of the De Beers Company, that prodigy which Rhodes guided in but a few years to the sole control of the diamond fields. He and Rhodes had lived and worked together, and had spent what leisure hours came to them riding in the veld, spinning their dreams of the new country in the north.

In 1884 Pickering was thrown from his horse and suffered internal injuries. For two years he lay dying, and Rhodes, with Jameson called in as the doctor, nursed him with untiring devotion. When the end was near, it happened that Rhodes had gone off to the great new gold reef that had been found in the Transvaal. Always in the forefront of business deals in Africa, Rhodes secured two options, one on the farm of Hans Du Plessis, the other on the farm known as Doornfontein. For the first he would have to pay five hundred pounds, and since that date more than a hundred million pounds worth of gold has been dug from the farmland. Doornfontein would have cost him but half the price, and only two years later its municipal valuation was three million pounds. To-day, of course, it is infinitely more valuable, as it is now slum property in the heart of Johannesburg.

But before the options fell due, Jameson sent a message. Pickering was sinking. Rhodes hurried back to Kimberley on the mail-cart sitting on the mail bags on the long dusty journey, for there was no other room—and stayed, never moving from Pickering's side, during the final weeks. He ignored telegrams from Johannesburg, if he ever noticed they arrived, and the options lapsed. It was October, stiflingly hot and airless in the unpretentious little house of corrugated iron where Pickering fought his last battle for air, as Rhodes was to fight it in Muizenberg sixteen years later, still a comparatively young man. Pickering was hardly more than a boy, and he died in Rhodes' arms at one o'clock in the morning whispering, "You have been father, mother, brother and sister to me." That same day Rhodes left the house and moved across to live with Jameson.

By then both Rhodes and Jameson were thirty-three. As a living companion Rhodes was apt to be a trifle intense. He was at the climax of his fight to amalgamate the Kimberley diamond mines under his own control, an accomplishment that was to be but incidental to his plans "to acquire a country and form an empire", as the trust deed of the De Beers Company so modestly proposed.

Rhodes' meal-time conversation, carried on into the small hours, tended to repeat itself. He had a habit, when he hit on an idea, or a sounding phrase, of saying it over and over again, and after two years, Jameson was unlikely altogether to have missed the drift of what he was getting at. It was all talk of the north—" the balance of the map". But to Jameson the problem of opening up Africa to the north was purely academic. His interests and ambitions were concerned with the wealthy invalids of Kimberley, and then Vienna. He even treated the empire-builder's dreams irreverently, which was mainly why Rhodes kept on repeating them.

Then Frank Thompson fled from Bulawayo and Rhodes' schemes were in jeopardy. Moreover, the money and the rifles promised in the Concession had soon to be delivered to Lobengula if the King were to be kept to his contract. On an impulse, Rhodes asked Jameson to take a holiday and " fill the vacuum " in Bulawayo, and the doctor, with an alacrity that surprised himself as much as Rhodes, left his practice the very next day to the mercies of a recently acquired junior partner.

In the next fifteen months, between February 1889 and May 1890, Jameson made three journeys to Bulawayo. He was a city-bred man, although over the last ten years he had shed any urban affectation that might have been left to him, in the inelegant democracy of the diamond diggings. Even so, his background was hardly such as to suggest that he was the ideal person to undertake a journey of more than seven hundred miles each way through trackless country as wild as its savage inhabitants. By ox-wagon the round journey took four months. On the third trip, in April 1890, when a more than usual urgency prevailed, he rode on horseback to Bulawayo in seventeen days, which was a creditable feat for a townsman. In time, these three journeys, exceeding in all four thousand miles, were to appear but an insignificant part of his travels through the continent. But, in February 1889, the prospect was something of an adventure and he set off with little idea of what the next few years were to bring him.

The old road—such as it was—to Bulawayo from Kimberley, through Mafeking, followed generally the route of the present railway to Rhodesia, skirting the border of the Transvaal. For many months of the year this part of the continent is arid. But, when spring comes, the thorn bush and msasa trees turn verdant green, without any apparent source of moisture to encourage them. Down by the river beds, when the streams start running after the first rains, mimosa comes out in its gay yellow blossom, and sometimes its sweet scent drowns even the stifling smell of dust that usually besets the traveller.

In those days there was the occasional suspicion of a track, where a previous traveller had passed. But the untamed veld soon blotted out any path not constantly in use, especially when the rains came and the rank grass spread like a flame.

The road passed through Bechuanaland, climbing all the time to the higher veld. All this country in southern Africa is what is technically known as " savannah ", although there are few people in the continent who use the word or even understand what it means. South of the Zambesi, the bush is seldom thick. In parts, there are open grassy plains, but generally the land, broken by steep but shallow kopjes, is covered with stunted trees.

Overlooked from a distance, the land appears wooded but the trees are, in fact, sparsely scattered. As a man walks through the bush, the trees seem all the time to thicken in a ring round him, as if he were himself the centre of a partial clearing. As he moves on, the clearing moves with him and the circle of thicker bush, a hundred yards or so in radius, moves too. The truth is that the bush is never very thick but stretches mile after mile without a break, and in perspective the farther trees seem more densely packed. Often, the veld is flat and featureless, and there is little to dispel the illusion that one is passing the same stunted thorn trees over and over again. As there is a danger of walking in a circle and doing this very thing—particularly when the midday sun is almost directly overhead—a journey through the bush has its problems.

So the city-bred little doctor bumped along in his ox-wagon through hundreds of miles of country empty of all civilized habitation. There were certainly human dwellings occasionally to be seen, but these, and their occupants —who leapt out brandishing spears and dressed to look as terrifying as possible—were hardly reassuring to a stranger. Not that Jameson ever suffered undue concern over native savages. The white man in Africa to-day goes about in much greater fear of his black brother than Jameson ever knew, if only because, unlike Jameson, he has lost faith in his own superiority. His fear to-day may be more moral than physical, but it is fear nevertheless. Jameson rode into the wilds of Africa as he marched into the wards of University College Hospital, with "masterly and humorous benevolence", which went down just as well with the Matabele warrior as with the Cockney labourer because, appearances notwithstanding, they both belonged to the same human race—whose two universal attributes are respect for mastery, and a sense of the ridiculous.

Thus came Jameson to Bulawayo, and he sat himself down on the goats' dung in front of Lobengula where, instead of flattering the King, he made him laugh. He had another advantage over the other white men who sought so hard to ingratiate themselves with Lobengula. He had a box of instruments and a cabinet of medicines, and he practised a witchcraft of his own that met with the King's approval because it was so constantly effective.

Fortunately the King had a chronic complaint, giving Jameson a ready-made chance to show his powers. Lobengula suffered from gout, because he ate raw meat and drank copiously of rough beer and took no exercise. When his attacks became too painful, he had been in the habit of calling his own witch doctors to search out among his subjects, and put to death, the person who was obviously causing him such distress. By delaying their choice of a suitable victim until the precise moment when the bout showed signs of easing off, the doctors proved their efficacy.

In the interests of local humanity, Jameson sought to convince Lobengula that the royal body was above human influence, a new and attractive theory which, happily for his subjects, the King eagerly accepted. Jameson suggested that if proper witchcraft were employed, such as was fit and meet only for Kings, the results would be beyond all expectations. But it must have taken courage to persuade a savage king in the presence of a bodyguard of fanatics, handily armed with stabbing assegais, to submit the royal person to the jab of a hypodermic needle, often in the seat of regal dignity. Jameson succeeded, because he made the King laugh about it.

Jameson stayed but ten days in Bulawayo on his first visit and then set out on the long trip south back to Kimberley. For the time being, the vacuum had been filled. New men were left at the kraal as watchdogs of Rhodes' interests. Jameson returned to his practice undisturbed, for Rhodes was in England negotiating the royal Charter which was to give the Queen's blessing to that prodigy of his dreams, the British South Africa Company.

Four months later, in August, Lobengula was reported to be growing fractious again and once more Jameson agreed to fill the breach. Another two months' journey through the scrub and sand drifts of Bechuanaland, and he was back with the King propitiating him with banter and occasional shots of morphia. There was a second object to his visit this time. It was necessary to get some men actually digging for gold in the country lest it might appear that the Concession had been extracted from Lobengula merely as a blind for some less innocent purpose—a suggestion that would have been dangerously near the truth. It took Jameson six weeks to persuade the King to honour his side of the contract and permit digging to start. Loben-

gula had been ready enough to take the money Jameson
had brought—which he did not want, anyway, because it
was of no value to him—although, with typical native
sophistry, he refused to accept the rifles which he wanted.
By some perverted process of thought, he believed he was
thus injuring the white men.

Jameson remained in Matabeleland for four months,
until the middle of February 1890. During that time he
made two trips to Tati goldfields and was able to report to
Rhodes that digging at least had been started. In the
intervals, when the first differences had been overcome,
his influence with Lobengula grew and the King made him
one of his indunas, of which office the main badges of
rank were a pair of ox-tail garters and a monkey-skin that
had been inadequately cured.

It was during Jameson's sojourn in Bulawayo on this occasion that the Queen sent a mission of British Guardsmen
to pay her gracious respects to her contemporary, the King
of the Matabele, and, incidentally, to break the news to
him as gently as possible, that she had granted a Charter
to the British South Africa Company which empowered
the Company, in her name, to occupy Lobengula's land.

The Charter was an imposing document with little rela-
tion to the modest objectives of the original Rudd Concession on which it was supposed to have been based. It gave
the Company authority to do virtually anything it wanted,
almost as a sovereign power in its own land. The import
of some of its provisions would have surprised Lobengula if
he had been able to understand them. In almost the first
paragraph it mentioned as one of its objectives the regula-
tion of liquor traffic with the natives—just at a time when
Lobengula and his wives were acquiring a lively taste for
champagne. There followed a pious resolution to suppress
the slave-trade, of whose existence in the country there was
no evidence at all.

The mission of guardees arrived in Bulawayo in January

at the height of the rains and the hottest season of the year. It consisted of a major, a captain and a corporal-major of the Royal Horse Guards, in a four-wheeled coach painted red and yellow—with the royal monogram and crown in gold. After a sodden journey of thirteen hundred miles from the coast, through the storm-swept African continent, the mission's appearance at Lobengula's kraal in full ceremonial dress—blue coats, breastplates, shining helmets, horsehair plumes and top boots—was a military accomplishment of no mean order.

The mission carried a message from the Queen, composed with consummate care by a distinguished gentleman in Whitehall who probably had never seen a black man outside a minstrel show. Jameson read it through before the ceremony of presenting it to Lobengula, and pronounced it "unintelligible rubbish". He re-wrote it himself in the style Lobengula would like to hear and thus was delivered to the King of the Matabele a supposed official communication from Her Britannic Majesty Queen Victoria. There is no record of what was in Jameson's version, which, for the sake of the lasting dignity of the British Crown is, perhaps, fortunate. But as Lobengula seemed to accept the situation and the Charter resignedly, it can be assumed that its purport was very different from what Whitehall had gone to such trouble to convey to him.

Jameson's first hurdle, to persuade Lobengula to allow men to start digging for gold he did not want himself anyway, had only taken six weeks to surmount, which showed it had been a relatively simple negotiation. But it was a different problem to win the King's enthusiastic consent to a white army intruding in his "principalities and dominions" north of the Limpopo. Not that Jameson was unequal to it. Perhaps Lobengula's new complaint of sore eyes gave him an unfair advantage, for it is always difficult for a man to gainsay his doctor.

The Charter had given Rhodes his own Queen's authority

to occupy Mashonaland, and he had every intention of using his powers in the widest sense. Jameson's task was to persuade Lobengula, as the sovereign king, that an invasion of his country by armed white men—who were wont to assume airs of aggressive superiority even when they were unarmed—was of such inoffensive intent that he should welcome it. It was true, as Jameson said, that the white men had no wish to enter Matabeleland itself and would merely skirt Lobengula's country on their way to Mashonaland, although this nice distinction between two undefined territories had been conveniently overlooked in the Rudd Concession, which had named Lobengula king of them both.

The measure of Jameson's influence over the hesitant King was shown by the way Lobengula's consent to this new idea was rushed through, as it were, in two short months. Jameson prevailed on him, not only to agree to let the white men pass, but to promise to send a hundred labourers into the bargain to help to cut a road for the invaders through the trackless Matabele country.

In April, Jameson was back in Kimberley, where Rhodes and his lieutenants were already organizing a force to occupy Mashonaland. The possibility of Jameson settling down once more to his practice was now remote.

Among the unique personalities that Rhodes had gathered round him was a hunter, Frank Selous, who knew more than any other white man about the interior of the Zambesi country. It had been eighteen years before—when most of the Matabele had never set eyes on a white man—when Selous had first asked Lobengula for permission to shoot game. Lobengula could see little menace in the slim young figure, and had said, "Go where you will, you are only a boy."

Selous had gone where most other men feared to go and, surprisingly, had survived, which was more than could be said for most of the wild beasts, particularly elephants, he had come across. His knowledge of the country was invaluable in opening up new trails, and Rhodes sent him north to meet the labourers Lobengula had promised. They were to come to Palapye, about half-way between Kimberley and Bulawayo, but when Selous arrived there was no sign of them. An extra two or three hundred miles was nothing to him, so he pushed on to Bulawayo in an impatient mood.

He was now no more the suppliant youth. He had lived in the veld on his own for so long he had become intolerant of other humans. Not unnaturally, he upset the royal dignity, and in a few hours Jameson's painful work of months was undone. Lobengula, ever since he had undertaken to help cut the road, had been waiting for a chance to deny it. He had once said, "there is a wall round the word of a chief", but it was only since he had been dealing with the white men that he got the chance—by making statements he never intended and then denying them—to express what he really meant. Now he asserted there was no need to send labourers to cut a road as he had no intention of permitting a white impi to march into his country.

Sharp words often lose their sting when passed through an interpreter. Unfortunately, Selous spoke Lobengula's tongue and none of his meaning was lost. He denounced the King's integrity and person. In response, Lobengula railed at the name of Rhodes who, he said, was nothing but a myth. If Rhodes really existed, why had he never shown the courage to come and see him?

"Go back," the King said to Selous, "and take Rhodes by the hand and bring him here."

The image of a long, lean, bearded hunter trudging hand in hand with the burly Rhodes through the eternal thorn bush of Bechuanaland may be intriguing to us. To Selous it was merely irritating. He left Lobengula in disgust and hurried back to Kimberley—just another little jaunt of seven hundred miles—where his report threw Rhodes' camp into consternation.

Jameson secretly relished the development. It was clear now he was the only one capable of dealing with Lobengula and it gave him a comforting feeling of indispensability. In a letter to his brother, saying that he might have to go back to Bulawayo to relieve the situation, he said, " It will be as a favour and distinctly requested."

For the third time Rhodes " distinctly requested " him to go and " fill the vacuum ". In a breathless dash on horseback Jameson made the journey to Bulawayo in seventeen days. Once more he sat on the goats' dung under the indaba tree and faced Lobengula. The King was in an unusually petulant mood. He was beginning to see whither the white men's schemes were leading him and his people. He drew for Jameson the picture of the chameleon which, having changed its colour to merge with its surroundings, stalks a fly with slow jerky movements, rocking backwards and forwards slightly on its feet, always rocking a little more forward than backward so that its advance to the fly is imperceptible until, within range, it shoots out its fantastically long tongue with an annihilating flick, and the fly is eaten up.

" England," said Lobengula, " is the chameleon, and I am the fly." It was a perfect analogy, even truer than he really knew. If Jameson had been anyone else there was little he could have done to gainsay it.

Even so, with all his blandishments, when at last Jameson left Bulawayo, it was not with Lobengula's enthusiastic blessing. Their last interview took place early one morning, just as Jameson set off for the south. He caught the King at the door of his house, in *déshabillé*. Stark naked, black and fat as his sacred cattle, Lobengula leaned over the lower half of the door.

Jameson, with the moral advantage of the clothed, said, " Since you will not give me the road as you promised,

I will bring my white impi and if necessary we will fight."

Lobengula demurred. This was dangerous talk. "I have never refused you the road," he said grudgingly.

"Very well," said Jameson, "then you acknowledge you have promised to grant me the road and unless you refuse now your promise holds good."

The King shuffled awkwardly behind the door and made no reply.

"Good-bye, Chief," said Jameson. "You have given me your promise and on the strength of that promise I will bring my impi."

Jameson set off once more down the long road to Mafeking and Kimberley, leaving the flies and the goats' dung, the persevering smell of the rubbish heap, and the bones of the slaughtered cattle. They were the trappings of a moribund court.

The two men, between whom there had grown up a strange mutual respect, never met again. When Jameson next came to Bulawayo, three years later, the camp and the goat kraal were a heap of smouldering ruins and Lobengula had fled northwards to his wretched death.

V

THE military people who knew all about campaigning in Africa told Rhodes it would take a force of two thousand five hundred men to occupy Mashonaland. As the only way they knew into the country was straight up the old hunters' road through Bulawayo, which Lobengula would be sitting astride with a trained army of thirty thousand warriors or more, their estimate of the military strength required was fairly sanguine. Even with rifles and machine-guns, twenty-five hundred white men, beset by the strange privations of the veld, would be little match for a horde of savages thoroughly at home in bush fighting and exceeding ten times their number.

Fully apprised of these professional considerations, Rhodes proposed to undertake the expedition with two hundred and fifty.

It was a young man named Frank Johnson who hit on this particular number, quite at random. By a chance that was to decide the entire future history of a country—to say nothing of his own—he took breakfast at the Kimberley Club on the morning of 22nd December 1889. He had been prospecting for gold in the wild country to the north and had arrived in town early that day from Bulawayo where he had recently faced an inconvenient charge by the Matabele of murder. One of the headmen assigned to him by Lobengula as an escort on his journeys had died of fever after Johnson had tried to cure him by dosing him with quinine. The awkward fact that Johnson had suffered from fever too at the time, and had taken the medicine him-

self and survived, was incontrovertible evidence of witchcraft practised at the expense of the lamented headman.
Lobengula himself would have liked to drop the charge, for
it had embarrassing possibilities and he was too frightened
of the white men's obvious power to risk their displeasure by
any rash action against one of them. At the same time he
had to keep quiet the young warriors who were beginning
to resent the white men's growing intrusion into their
country. After a long drawn-out trial at the royal court,
Johnson was solemnly sentenced to put back where he had
found it all the gold he had taken from the country. History is silent as to how, or even whether, any attempt was
made to promulgate the sentence, but the convicted man
had arrived that morning in Kimberley without any
apparent signs of restraint.

Frank Johnson, like Cecil Rhodes, was born in Norfolk
and had come to South Africa to seek a fortune at the
advanced age of sixteen. Inconsiderately, the bank in Cape
Town, to enter whose service he had travelled many thousands of miles, failed just before he arrived. In fact, there
were a number of commercial failures in Cape Town that
year and Johnson grasped a heaven-sent opportunity—not
for the last time in his life—and joined the fire brigade
which, being in heavy demand, was offering unusually good
pay. When the temporary depression in commerce had
abated, the pay was summarily decreased, so he enlisted in
a mounted unit and went north to Bechuanaland.

For some reason known only to the army, which guards
the secrets of its reasoning jealously, they made him a
quartermaster-sergeant. In this exalted rank he presumably learned something about provisioning troops, so he
cannot be dismissed as altogether unqualified for the task he
was given, some years later, of undertaking the entire
organization of the force that was to occupy Mashonaland.
Not that his army experience was unduly prolonged. In a
couple of years he was out, prospecting for gold in the

Zambesi country and founding the fortune of what was later to be known as the Bechuanaland Exploration Company—which carried out most of its exploring outside Bechuanaland—and is one of the largest property-owners in Matabeleland to-day.

Johnson's travels had taken him as far north in Lobengula's country as any white man, and his persistent search for gold had caused the Matabele to look on him with justifiable suspicion. The affair over the headman had been the highlight of a boisterous excursion. By the 22nd December 1889, when he sat down to breakfast at the Kimberley Club, he was a veteran of twenty-four and, unlike most of the adventurous spirits of the day, had an acknowledged wife and child in Cape Town.

Rhodes, whom he had met but briefly once before, came quite by chance and sat at his table. Rhodes had just received the military estimate for the Mashonaland expedition. The pay alone for a force of two and a half thousand men for the period of the invasion would cost more than the whole paid-up capital of the Company. To a business man this was a far more serious consideration than the strength of the Matabele. Rhodes, who was thirty-six, looked depressed, and Johnson, in deference to advanced age, felt it his duty to put a cheerful face on things at the breakfast table.

"Absurd," he said, with the assurance of one knowing well what he was talking about. "With two hundred and fifty men I would walk through the country."

As he later confessed, for all he knew about it he might just as well have said twenty-five. He could hardly have given the problem much serious thought. He knew neither where the force was to go, nor what it was expected to do when it got there. Five minutes before, he had not even known it was projected.

Rhodes was so impressed by his obvious grasp of the situation that he accepted his judgment on the instant and from then on the empire-builder's plans to pioneer this new country in the heart of darkest Africa were evolved from Johnson's inspired guess.

Between mouthfuls of bacon and eggs Rhodes asked, "How much will it cost?" This was the all-important question, and it was clear he valued Johnson's opinion. He was never very sure about gradations of military rank, and as someone had told him Johnson had been a quartermaster-sergeant Rhodes naturally believed he knew all about paying and provisioning armies.

Johnson, for his part, was certain of it. His assurance unabated, he said, "Give me the use of a room and plenty of paper and by lunch time I will let you know." He retired to the quietest corner the club could offer, and at midday he presented Rhodes with an estimate of nearly ninety thousand pounds sterling. Thus, the planning staff of one had, in a few hours, worked out the logistics of the whole military operation of adding a new country to the Empire.

The idea, unwittingly conceived by Johnson, of putting the occupation of Mashonaland out to contract, appealed to Rhodes. The alternative was to hand it over to the soldiers, who would search out all the attractive military possibilities inherent in the campaign and make it as long and costly as they could. The difference between a soldier's and a contractor's approach to the business would be that the soldier would go looking for a fight—and the promotion and ribbons to be gained from it—while the contractor would go out of his way to avoid one lest it should diminish his profits.

Rhodes offered the contract to Johnson. After a series of becoming refusals, like a coy bride, he submitted.

In our modern and more enlightened world, when all capitalistic enterprise is suspect, even among the capitalists themselves, a concern like the Chartered Company would be expected to procure at least two competitive tenders before committing itself to the expenditure of a round hundred thousand pounds. In any case it would require a contract to be sealed by a legal agreement drawn up by its attorneys. Johnson certainly concluded an agreement with Rhodes, who acted on behalf of the Company, but he drew it up himself and Rhodes signed it with but a perfunctory glance through it. To-day, a transaction on but one-tenth the scale would involve endless conferences and board meetings and interchange of minutes—without these there might be little to justify the existence of the directors, and their handsome fees.

On the morning of the first of January 1890, Johnson wrote out the contract with his own hand and Rhodes signed it the same evening and gave him a cheque for thirty thousand pounds as an advance. The Company's solicitors in London, disturbed to learn that a contract of such magnitude had been given out without incurring any lawyers' fees, cabled demanding to know what security Rhodes had obtained from the contractor.

Rhodes replied shortly, "Have got security—his life," and there the matter rested.

Surprisingly enough, the contract was quite a business-like document. Johnson undertook in it to construct a good wagon road all the way from Palapye in Bechuana-land to what had been christened Mount Hampden, a prominent hill which he had once seen himself, some four hundred miles to the north. The road would swing on a wide arc whose centre was Bulawayo, and along its whole length it would never be less than a hundred and fifty miles from Lobengula's kraal. The military would have been loath to make such an indirect approach to Mashona-land. It would have savoured too much of avoiding a fight.

Johnson would pay the whole cost of the expedition except for the provision of arms and ammunition, which Rhodes would have to buy himself. He would build a fort at Mount Hampden, when he got there, and he would guard the country against the entry of hostile forces—a fairly sanguine undertaking which, luckily for him, he was never called on to honour. In addition to the globular sum, for those days, of ninety thousand pounds—it would be worth much more than double to-day—he would receive a grant of land in Mashonaland of a mere eighty thousand acres. In his autobiography written fifty years later, Johnson reveals how careless he must have been over details, because he says he cannot remember ever having taken over the land. However, it was a generous gesture on the part of the Company—if they ever actually knew it was in the contract—because their concession from Lobengula had given them no rights to the land, which belonged to the Mashonas anyway.

When the soldiers heard that Rhodes planned to enter the country with a handful of civilians led by a contractor, like a road gang, their professional susceptibilities were seriously hurt. If the few unclaimed countries left in the world were to be annexed by a lot of amateurs, they would soon find themselves out of work. They brought pressure to bear in high places and, much against his will, Rhodes was compelled to agree that his two hundred and fifty pioneers must be turned into soldiers, even if only for the duration of the invasion. His idea was that the men who were to march into Mashonaland should be the first of the future citizens of the new country that was to be added to the British Empire, and they were to be recruited with that end in view. They would be farmers, miners, builders, butchers, tailors, doctors, clergymen and, against his better inclinations, lawyers. In the end he reduced the number to two hundred. As a true South African, a community of white men without its quota of native labour was beyond even his vision, so he replaced the extra fifty with three times the number of natives, who would cost about the same. The matter of cost was an all-important factor.

The two hundred white men were to be attested as soldiers, their ranks would be stiffened by regular officers, and Johnson himself as the commanding officer would be given the local rank of major. By making him the senior ranking officer he would be ensured his profits.

Even so, the quasi-military flavour of the expedition was not martial enough for the higher authorities. Not unreasonably, they insisted that amateur soldiers might need some more experienced protection in the depths of an uncharted continent teeming with war-like savages. When Rhodes announced he had no intention of leaving behind any line of communication—for, as he said, his pioneers would be a self-contained community, provisioned for many months ahead and not requiring lines of supply—they openly doubted his sanity and threatened to cancel the Charter. Under this high-handed compulsion he gave in, but with bad grace, for he was suspicious of the soldiery, and in any case it was he who had to foot the bill. They insisted on an escort of five hundred police—or, so they were to be called, although they were to be armed to the teeth—and a series of forts was to be built along the line of march. Men were to be left to garrison each fort—unproductive mouths to feed, as Rhodes saw them. The police were to be commanded by an experienced officer, Colonel Pennefather of the Inniskilling Dragoons.

The inclusion in the expedition of a regular colonel, ranking higher than the contractor who was charged with delivering it to its destination, raised a nice point of military responsibility. The pioneers themselves were under Johnson's command, and the police under Pennefather were primarily a separate escort. But in an emergency in the bush the whole force would need to act as a unit and the Colonel's rank would automatically place him in control. A situation could arise where the two leaders might differ, for although the colonel held the rank, it was the major who held the money bags. Military considerations might dictate a wide deviation from the route; economic necessity—that is, whether it would involve loss to the contractor—might discourage it. The pioneers whom the colonel would be ordering were not paid by his Queen, but by one of his junior officers. Whose would be the decision?

In a characteristic way Rhodes solved the problem, or so he believed. He sent his friend Jameson to go along with the column, without any official standing, but holding his power of attorney. Jameson was in effect but a civilian camp follower. Not that the lack of rank would deter him from assuming high military authority, as history was to prove. But the theory was that if the commanding officer and the contractor came to cross purposes, Jameson would step in and, in Rhodes' name, agree—or not—to pay any extra cost occasioned by military exigencies. Thus he was to be the final arbiter and, because of that, he assumed an aura of leadership in the expedition that was never intended. It is typical of Rhodes that the only difficulties he foresaw were over money. Jameson's position in the event of a clash of personalities was never defined. The power of attorney could have had little influence over sheer obstinacy.

Not that any disputes did arise between the two commanders. It is perhaps unfortunate for the military student that this theory of command was never fully tested, for had it been successful it might have revolutionized the principles of war—and the civilized world might well have adopted the method of sending armies into battle under contract, led gallantly by a managing director commissioned by the shareholders.

It was part of Johnson's contract to recruit the pioneers. While they were to represent a variety of trades and professions so that they could make up the nucleus of a population, Rhodes insisted that a fair number should come from the best South African families. Not that he was at all concerned with their birth and breeding. He was merely insuring against the discomforting possibility of his column being attacked and wiped out by the Matabele. To him, it was a far cheaper form of insurance than military protection that might not be wanted anyway. If the Matabele were to fall on a band of obscure adventurers—good fellows though they might be—the public would laud them as heroes, and might even subscribe a few guineas to a memorial in one of the London squares, but the hopes of the Charter would have been shattered and all the money spent on the expedition wasted. On the other hand, if the unfortunate victims could include a few sons of the oldest South African families—who had had this sort of trouble with black men before—the uproar would be so loud that the imperial authorities would be shamed into sending another expedition to extract retribution from the wicked Matabele, perhaps even at their own expense. Then the Matabele would be overthrown properly and the worthy objects of the Charter happily achieved, and B.S.A. Company shares would soar. It may be that Lobengula realized all this, for in the event he left the column discreetly alone, which saved the Imperial Government a deal of money, and obliged the Company to fight the Matabele War at its own expense three years later.

The pioneers were recruited at Kimberley and Mafeking and from these towns were marched to their training point, Camp Cecil, on the northern bank of the Limpopo. In actual fact, the white men who went north into the Zambesi country with the 1890 column never crossed the Limpopo. They passed round to the west of its headwaters. But they still had three of its tributaries to cross, the Macloustie, the Shashi and the Nuanetsi. It was at Macloustie, on the river of that name, that the British South Africa Company's police—forerunners of the B.S.A. Police of to-day—were assembling. The two assembly camps, of pioneers and police, were kept deliberately apart to avoid disaffection, for the potent reason that the pioneers were being paid more than the police.

At Camp Cecil the adventurous spirits of the pioneers were tamed by a course of military training lasting nearly two months, and Johnson drummed into them a high standard of discipline, after which the two sections of the invading army were considered sufficiently conditioned to be brought together safely at Macloustie.

Here they were inspected by a real live general, Lord Methuen, of the Cape Command. He had the officers called together and, in his best staff-college manner, addressed them with a gravity fitting the occasion. About to start on adventure into the unknown, they must be adequately briefed.

"Gentlemen," said his lordship, "have you got your maps?"

They brought out their sheets of cloth claiming to represent the uncharted country to the north.

"And pencils?" he asked courteously. Pencils were somehow produced.

"Then, gentlemen, your destination is Mount Hampden." They had known this for six months. He went on, "You first go to a point marked Siboutsi. I do not know whether Siboutsi is a man or a mountain. Mr. Selous, I understand, is of the opinion that it is a man, but we will pass that by. Then you get to Mount Hampden. Mr. Selous is of the opinion that Mount Hampden is placed ten miles too far to the west. You had better correct that." A rustle and marking of maps. "Perhaps, on second thought, better not. Because you might possibly be placing it ten miles too far to the east. Good morning, gentlemen."

After which heartening exhortation, the force—seven hundred white men, a couple of hundred natives, a hundred and seventeen wagons with two thousand oxen to drag them—crossed the Macloustie into Lobengula's country.

The next obstacle was the Shashi river, not twenty miles

ahead.   Here the column formed its first of many laagers and here came the first sign of interest in its movements from the Matabele.   A dozen warriors, in ostrich feathered regimentals, with ugly-looking assegais, came brazenly into the camp with a message from Lobengula.

One of the traders in Bulawayo had written the message at Lobengula's dictation.   Its tone of diplomatic impudence showed a distinct trace of Jameson's influence on the King.

"Has the King killed any white men that an impi is on the border," it ran, adding artlessly, "or have the white men lost something they are looking for?"

The letter deserved a better reply than it received, but someone other than Jameson answered it, lamely pleading that the force of nearly a thousand men was only a working party, protected by a few soldiers.

This little working party, with its meagre escort, boasted the finest scale of rations and equipment that, up to that time, had ever been issued to a field force in the Empire. There was little of the freebooter about the pioneers, in their brown corduroy uniforms, yellow leather leggings, bush hats and waterproof coats.   They were mounted on horses guaranteed immune from horse sickness.   Johnson had jibbed at buying salted horses; they were more expensive than he had bargained for.   That is one of the military disadvantages of campaign by contract.   But Rhodes was founding a new country and his horses were as essential as his pioneers, so he agreed to pay the difference.   The men carried Martini-Henry rifles in gun-buckets, Webley revolvers in holsters at their waists, and long-handled axes slung across the saddle.   They were paid seven and six a day— while the unfortunate policemen only got five shillings— and at the end of the journey they were to receive a grant of three thousand acres each, of land the Company did not own, and the right to peg fifteen mining claims.   There was certainly an impi on the border looking for something, as Lobengula protested. But whatever it was they were looking for, it was he himself who had lost it.

It was on the eleventh of July 1890 that the column crossed the Shashi into Matabeleland. They built Fort Tuli on the north bank of the river and the first garrison was left in charge. It was, perhaps, a little extravagant to call it a fort, but its earth bank might afford some protection against attack. The next two hundred miles of march lay through the thick bush of the low veld and it was here the real danger from the Matabele lay.

The rate of advance was twelve miles a day at the most. One pioneer troop would go ahead cutting down trees— hacking out the stumps to let the wagons pass—and Selous's scouts would ride out fanwise to look out for Matabele, and sometimes get terrifyingly lost.

The long line of wagons stretched for two miles and, in the event of a surprise attack, would take at least a couple of hours to concentrate. Standing one morning on a hill, looking down at the column as it snaked its way through mile after mile of potential ambush, seeing it in all its vulnerability for the first time, Johnson had a bad moment. From then on, he halved its length and made the column move forward on two parallel tracks. The work of road cutting was doubled, but the reduction in anxiety made it well worth while.

It was the Bamangwato chief Khama—who had embraced Christianity but had no love for his neighbour Lobengula —who lent Rhodes the hundred and fifty native labourers for the column. The missionaries had taught these people godliness but not, as yet, cleanliness. It was hot and sticky in the low veld, although it was mid-winter, and the pioneers found the smell of the natives unpalatable. The pious Bamangwato reported that the white men's language was even more offensive. By mutual consent black and white parted company at the Lundi river and the Bamangwato went back to the comforts of their missions.

On the way out they played one Christian prank. Having left the column early in the morning they reappeared at midday apparently in acute distress, saying two thousand Matabele were on their tails. The column laagered as best it could in a bad defensive position and some confusion. In the excitement the Bamangwato melted inconspicuously away and it was not until the next morning that the column faced the truth and relaxed. Unfortunately for the Bamangwato, they were then too far away to savour the full effect of their little joke.

At the Lundi river another message came from Lobengula. "Go back at once and take your young men," he said, "or I will not be answerable for the consequences." He was sincere enough himself in his hope to avoid a fight, but he feared his inability to keep his warriors from taking their own initiative. But it was not a heartening message to receive when there were still a hundred and fifty miles of thick bush country to hack through before the column would reach the open high veld.

Traditionally, the Zulus had always attacked just before dawn, and every morning from three o'clock till the sun came up the pioneers and their escort stood to, waiting for an enemy of whose probable tactics they knew nothing. In a flash of genius, Johnson had borrowed from the naval authorities at Simonstown a ten-thousand candlepower searchlight and he had mounted it on a wagon with a steam engine, dynamo and battery. All night long the great shaft of light stabbed the bush and, to heighten its magic, little land mines of gelignite, spread round the laager and fired from the battery, popped off like evil spirits.

There is no doubt that while Lobengula himself had the sense to see the ultimate futility of attacking the column—even though immediate victory would be certain—his warriors wanted to fight. All his regiments had massed spontaneously in Bulawayo and were clamouring for war and, most ominous sign of all, the women were busy making sandals for their men. It was only reports of the great rotating eye which saw even through the darkness, and was therefore pure witchcraft, that held the impis back. For, if the eye could see at night, it must be able all the more to search through the bush by day, and thus would spoil the whole Matabele way of attack which relied on being able to creep up on the enemy unobserved.

Day after day, ten, twelve miles at a time, the column struggled on, a tiny little island of white humanity in a sea of ominous unfriendliness. What good the garrison left behind at Fort Tuli, a hundred miles back, would have been if the Matabele attacked, only the military experts knew. Time and again in South African history the black men had shown they could wipe out well armed forces completely by sheer weight of numbers, leaving not even a survivor to tell how it had happened. For there were no such refinements as wounded or prisoners in a battle with savages. The Matabele were still to enjoy the taste of one of those annihilating victories, three years later, on the Shangani. The only reason they failed to wipe out the Rhodesian pioneer column while it still struggled through the low veld in the August days of 1890 was that they never attacked it.

VI

THE pioneer column climbed up to the high plateau which is the feature of Matabeleland, over what they named Providential Pass. As mountain passes go, one that takes eight miles to rise fifteen hundred feet hardly ranks as formidable. Napoleon's armies—who may have marched on their stomachs, but seldom on flat ground— would have climbed it as a matter of routine, ready to fight a battle at the top. The only real significance of Providential Pass was that it offered an easy way up an uninviting escarpment.

The hills rising from the low veld barred the column's way north, but Selous found a series of ridges that wound slowly to the top, and the oxen obligingly emulated the Grand Army and took them in their stride.

Over the top, the pioneers first saw the country they had set out to acquire for their own. The difference between the high and low veld of Africa is as the difference between light and shade. Down in the low veld, the bush is eternally still and unfriendly. Giant baobabs stand uncouth sentinels of its silent mysteries. Baobabs are not really trees at all, but monstrosities. A tree is a smiling creature, conscious of its own beauty. It stands firm and proud on lithe trunk and holds out friendly arms and waves welcoming fingers in the breeze. A baobab is grotesque—like a deformed freak, with horribly swollen trunk and shrivelled arms whose fingers curl up paralysed in sticky stagnant air.

For in the low veld there are no clean winds. The winds sweep clear over the tops of surrounding hills, and below them in the hollows the air moves sluggishly and unwillingly. Nor do refreshing rains sweep blithely across to wash the land. The rains that come in the fetid heat of summer fall vertically in unrelenting downpour until the veld stands marshy and sticky and, when at last a fierce sun breaks through, all the sodden evil steams up from a clammy earth.

But in the high veld, even in the tropics, the world is free and open with plains rolling to distant hills, blue at high noon and purple when the sun's rays fall and slant across them. On the high veld the bush is plentiful enough, but it is sparse, and wind and rain sweep cleanly through. In the open, where bush gives way to pasture, grass grows high and rivers splash merrily over sparkling rocks and bright washed sand. At least, that is what the country looks like at the ideal season of the year.

Yet in August, which was the month when the pioneers first saw it, the country does not always look so promising. August comes at the end of five months of drought, and there is at least another month to go before rain can be expected again. The grass, if not burnt up altogether, has by then been bleached almost white by the sun. The scraggy thorn bush has shed what sparse foliage it had, and the bush-veld, tramped out by cattle, is hard and bare. At that time of the year, the rivers are but occasional pools lying between stretches of dusty sand. In August and September the high veld looks anything but fertile. But the sun's rays are soft, the clear starlit nights crisp and, even though stark and leafless, the land seems to flow with milk and honey after the unfriendly desolation of the low veld.

That was how the pioneers felt about it, despite the unpromising look of the country after the dry months. When they reached the crest of the pass it was like emerging into a new world.

They stood as at the top of a flight of steps. Behind were

the trees, thickly covering the ground that fell away, gradually at first, then more steeply down the pass. In front was open country—park-like grassland dotted with spreading trees. To the right the ground rose slightly to a dark green range of hills, carpeted in trees, sending out a miniature mountain spur into the sunny distance. In front was level parkland, with a bold horizon of stately trees against the sky.

To the left the ground swept down to open plain—still parkland with its widely spaced trees—the grass across the plain bleached almost white. A mile or two away, still in the foreground of the picture, rose two grassy hills rounded like maidens' breasts, bright in the sunlight. Beyond them, at intervals, were more lines of rounded hills, each a little darker in the distance until, thirty miles away at least, a jagged black line of mountains stood up beyond the plain's unbroken horizon.

The pioneers stood and feasted their eyes on this new and inviting country, rejoicing that it was to be theirs. Their enthusiasm could also have sprung, not so much from relief—strong as it was—at being clear of the treacherous low veld, but from the certain knowledge, instilled unashamedly by those who had recruited them, that, when they really came to their destination among the tributaries of the Zambesi, they would find the headwaters of the rivers running over sands of sterling gold.

A few miles from the top of the pass they built their next fort and named it after their Queen. It was here at Fort Victoria but three years later that the shooting war with Lobengula was actually to break out, but the pioneers established it in the calm of a new-found security because at last they could see all around them and there was no longer constant fear of ambush. In fact, by the time the tail of the column struggled up over the top of the pass some men of the vanguard were already playing football, which was enough to prove to any watching Matabele that

the witchcraft practised by white men might be effective
but was remarkably undignified.

The rest of the journey, north from Fort Victoria, over
the open plains, was like a picnic after the struggle through
the low veld. Selous led them along the watershed from
which, on one side, the rivers run west and north to the
Zambesi and, on the other, east to the Sabi and the sea.
Even those headwaters that had to be crossed were but
shallow drifts at that time of the year.

A hundred miles farther on, they built another fort and
named it Fort Charter. It is the only one of the forts built
by the column in the country around which a town has not
grown. Here Selous and Jameson left the column to make
contact with a native chief in Manicaland, and so Jameson
started his epic journeys towards the sea, which is a story
we will come to later.

Johnson was not displeased to be free of Selous, who
tended to resent his authority. Johnson thought him a
supreme individualist, unamenable to discipline. He even
disparaged him as a guide because Selous wasted time with
technicalities like taking compass bearings in the trackless
veld. When Jameson asked, almost tentatively, if Selous
could be spared, Johnson surprised him by sitting down
without hesitation and writing out the peremptory order,
"Captain Selous, having resigned his commission this day,
is struck off the strength of the regiment accordingly."
Twenty-five years later, in 1915, the supreme individualist,
then over sixty, was killed in German East Africa, leading
his platoon as a second-lieutenant. Johnson, in his autobiography, graciously acknowledges the fallacy of hasty
judgments.

The column moved on quite competently with neither its
official guide nor its unofficial general. But any real danger
from the Matabele had by then been left behind and there
were now unlikely to be any causes of disagreement in the
command. Between the Umfuli and Hunyani rivers—

almost on the outskirts of what was to become the capital city of the country—five horses were eaten by lions and a trooper of the police spent an uncomfortable night up a tree while, below him, a lioness and her cubs made a leisurely meal of his mare. Otherwise, the last stages of the march were uneventful.

They were nearing the end of their journey now and at last they spotted the shape of Mount Hampden rising out of the plain to the north. They pushed on to the foot of the kopje where they outspanned and there proclaimed the township of Fort Salisbury, the capital of their new country formally annexed in the name of their Queen. Then someone climbed to the top and saw Mount Hampden still outlined unmistakably on the horizon. Selous had been right. Mount Hampden had been placed on their maps ten miles too far to the east and the hill they had come four hundred miles to find was not the one they had ceremoniously proclaimed as their destination.

It was on the thirteenth of September 1890 that Lieutenant Tyndale-Biscoe, R.N.—one of the sailors who had been seconded to the column to man the guns—hoisted the Union Jack on a crooked pole hastily cut from an unpromising selection of trees. It was fitting, of course, that a maritime people should choose a sailor to perform this historic office, but as the new country has never boasted a sea coast there was little future for the Navy in Rhodesia.

To-day, in place of the msasa pole there stands a straight and slender bronze flagstaff and round it bustles the precocious city of Salisbury. When the pioneers paraded in front of the flagpole, the ground was rough and the coarse September grass patchy. Where the troops formed up in lines, kicking their boots against patches of sand and rough stones, the sixty-year-old jacaranda trees of Cecil Square now spread their welcome shade, and at night a coloured fountain dispels the African darkness. In the background, where the wagons were outspanned and a rough and ready administration pitched its tents, the twentieth-century legislators now carry on the ordering of people's lives in more sumptuous establishments.

When Lieutenant Tyndale-Biscoe had secured the halyards to his satisfaction, Major Johnson read the orders for the day. The first was a fine piece of military punctilio. "It is notified for general information," it ran, "that the Column, having arrived at its destination, will halt." The next announced that all the land claimed by Lobengula in the Rudd Concession was annexed to the British Empire. As that very document had specifically named him King of that land, it is a nice constitutional point whether Lobengula was not, by Johnson's order, created a British sovereign.

A fortnight later, on the last day of September, the pioneers were paraded again. This time Johnson ordered, "Ground arms. Dismiss", and with a salute which could be interpreted by authority how it pleased, the men turned to the right and became civilians. Johnson's own feelings on losing his command were no doubt mollified by the seventeen and a half thousand pounds balance on his contract that immediately fell due.

Out into a country which was to be so often beset by drought, the pioneer settlers set forth on their quest for fortune and all but perished in the floods of the first rainy season. Nature, disappointed perhaps by Lobengula's spiritless failure, tried her best to drive the white men from the country. As gold fever quickly abated, the mosquitoes provided a ready substitute. From the start, the promised land of Ophir fell far short of expectations, and of the swarms of prospectors who had hurried off so eagerly to Mazoe and Hartley Hill, many came drifting back to Salisbury in the early months of 1891, fever-stricken and disillusioned. If the rivers ran over sands of gold, only drowned men would know it.

Yet so much had been said about the fortunes to be made

in Mashonaland that many others were ready and waiting to follow on the trail of the pioneers. Even before the column reached Salisbury, wagons were gathering on the banks of the Shashi. All they were waiting to hear was how Lobengula was reacting to the invasion. As soon as word came through that the column had reached Salisbury and established a fort, and the road to the south was linked by police posts, a great rush north started and a hundred and fifty wagons entered the country in November of 1890.

Then, once more, nature struck where the Matabele had hesitated. Like a Zulu impi, she waited in ambush until the white men reached the depths of the low veld. As if purposely to trap the intruders, rivers came down in flood, mosquitoes attacked in their swarms, and beside the road that the pioneers had cut unhindered between the Lundi and the Nuanetsi rivers, the first casualties of the occupation of Rhodesia were buried in their lonely graves. Men were washed down swollen rivers—they died in the delirium of blackwater fever—and, because they found themselves marooned between impassable floods, some even died of starvation.

In spite of all this, men continued to make their way north and the white population of the country steadily grew. When Rhodes first set foot in the country that was later to bear his name there were fifteen hundred white people in Salisbury. He entered the country from the east coast which was a more comfortable route, for it ran with the rivers and not across them. Not that it would have been a practicable line of approach for the pioneer column because the Portuguese, who had held the territory along the coast for hundreds of years, might well have objected to the passage of an army.

When Rhodes at last drove into Salisbury in a mule cart he was met, not by a jubilant welcome as father of a country, but by a Vigilance Committee primed with a catalogue of grievances. The spirit of the British people had been truly planted in the land.

The main trouble was over land titles. As an inducement to join the column the Chartered Company, with a lavish gesture, had promised three thousand acres of Mashonaland to each of the pioneers. Not that the Charter, or the Rudd Concession on which it was based, had ever for a moment suggested that the land of Mashonaland would be the Company's to give. But, on the face of it, this should not have been a serious obstacle, for the Company now occupied the land, and Lobengula and his Matabele, who were the only people who made any pretence to own it, had been virtually silenced by the column's display of force and witchcraft.

Taking a realistic view of the situation, it should only have been necessary to find a lawyer to draw up some impressive-looking title deeds and the land could have been made over to anyone to whom the Company felt like giving it. There should have been no difficulty about this for, despite Rhodes' prejudices, there were already plenty of lawyers in Mashonaland. In fact, the first partnership established after the dispersal of the column had been between two attorneys with the significant names of Bird and Hunter.

It was the lawyers themselves who obstinately refused this profitable solution to the difficulties. The pioneers wanted the land and the Company was quite willing to give it to them. The chance of raking in fees could never have been so gratuitously offered. But with typical legal perversity they discovered it was not as straightforward as it seemed. Lobengula had done a very clever thing.

Rhodes and the Company knew well enough that the Rudd Concession gave them no power in the land other than to enter it and dig for gold. Even Lobengula was unlikely to be so foolish as to give them more. Nor had Rhodes been so foolish as to ask for it. Getting what

Lobengula was prepared to give, he could take the rest without asking.

Or that is what he could have done if Lobengula had not been clever enough to give the rest to someone else who seemed in a better position than himself to keep it from Rhodes.

Immediately after Lobengula had signed the Rudd Concession and Rhodes' men had rushed triumphantly south with this doubtful proof of the King's grant of mineral rights, a German banker named Lippert had himself visited Lobengula. He was disappointed to find he had lost the race for the mineral rights, but he saw a chance to make something out of the trip, and took it. He assured Lobengula that, unlike the petty men who came from Rhodes, he was the fountain of his own wealth and showed him a thousand pounds in gold to prove it. This impressed Lobengula who had always harboured a certain doubt of the great Rhodes' actual existence.

Lippert offered the gold to Lobengula—and five hundred more pounds every year on top of it—for the whole of Lobengula's land. Lobengula still had no need, or even use, for the money but, knowing that Rhodes' people and Lippert's people were enemies—enemies like the Matabele and Zulus who would fight each other to the death rather than dwell in the same land—without a qualm he signed another concession giving Lippert what he asked. For if Rhodes had the right to dig for gold, and Lippert the right to own the land, they would fight and destroy each other and the land would remain for the Matabele people.

All this the lawyers had discovered—as lawyers so inconsiderately are apt to do—and, for a suitable fee, they advised the Company that the land could not be given away; not for the unimportant reason that the Company did not own it, but because of the inconvenient fact that someone else did.

Rhodes himself had never been very worried about Herr

Lippert and his concession. He had known all along what was going on. One of his guiding tenets was that every man has his price and he preferred the certainty of buying the rights of Lobengula's land from someone else, to the doubt of ever being able to wheedle it out of Lobengula himself. When he came to Salisbury and saw the mood and temper of the Vigilance Committee he thought it time to make the certainty an established fact.

The little sheet of paper, with Lobengula's illiterate cross, that Lippert had bought for a thousand pounds and the promise, never to be fulfilled, of more to come, cost the Chartered Company a million pounds. Three years after the Company was floated, its capital had to be doubled and the newly subscribed half went straight into the pocket of the German banker. At a time when every penny of the first million pounds was being spent on concentrated human effort to open up a new country, this second was squandered on a scrap of paper. But the pioneers got their titles to their land, and the Chartered Company fondly believed that it owned, in the fullest sense of the word, a country ten times the size of Wales.

Thirty years later, when the people of Rhodesia chose self-government, the Company was sharply disabused of this pleasant notion. On that occasion, four parties gathered to lay their claim to the land, like forgotten relatives inconveniently come back to challenge the disposal of an inheritance. The first was the Company itself, and confidently it produced the Lippert Concession as unquestionable proof that Lobengula, the rightful owner, had given the land to the holder of this grubby little document. The next were the natives, or what were left of them, but they had little valid claim beyond the fact that, until the white men came and took it away, the land had been indisputably theirs. The white settlers who now wanted, rather recklessly, to set up their own government, claimed the land by right of occupation.

Lastly, the Crown—the figurehead of the British people, who had stood back and watched the Company and settlers in their struggles and had themselves contributed nothing in money or effort—put in its claim and, not unnaturally, won.

Those who had bought land or had been given it by the Company were left to enjoy what they held. But the august House of Lords, sitting in judgment over the dispute, ruled that all the vast tracts of unoccupied land still left in the country belonged to the Crown. Their lordships held that only the Crown could lay claim to land by right of conquest. The empire-builders had gone out on their quests singing patriotic songs and flaunting the Union Jack, and annexing lands in the name of their Queen so, if they had thought at all about it, they could hardly have expected any other verdict. So the Crown took over the land and, somewhat ungraciously, accepted a rider that it should pay the Company three and three-quarter million pounds for the development work the Company had done. Ten years later the people of the newly constituted self-governing colony of Southern Rhodesia paid the Company another two million pounds for the mineral rights. Lobengula's clumsy cross, traced so laboriously and so grudgingly on the two concessions, had become one of the most valuable autographs in the world. In those days, six million pounds was a lot of money. And at last, after forty years without paying any dividends, Chartered shares came into their own.

When Lobengula heard that Rhodes had somehow acquired the land rights from Lippert, what little faith he had in white men passed right away. It fell to John Moffat, who at the time enjoyed the doubtful eminence of Resident Commissioner in Bulawayo, to break the news to the King.

It is said of Lobengula that, like all Zulu chiefs, he was a great gentleman. When Mr. Moffat discharged the embarrassing duty of telling him that Rhodes now owned both the gold and the land that held it, he pretended to take the news casually, as if it were of little consequence and went on chatting to those around him.   But a cold hand had clutched at his heart, which for a moment stopped beating, and, great bull of a man that he was, he felt faint.   Nothing of this showed through the dark mahogany of his skin, and he would never have allowed to be known what he felt inside.   Without a sign that the news had come like a death sentence, he went on talking to Mr. Moffat, still the essence of royal urbanity and tremendous dignity.

When, at last, the Resident Commissioner had withdrawn, the full horror of what was happening flooded over him like a deluge as he saw, so clearly and unmistakably, the English chameleon rocking mercilessly towards him, ready now at any moment to flick out its tongue and devour him and his people like a miserable fly.   His fear flamed to anger and from that day on he swore to drive the white intruders from his land.

VII

I T needed no profound sagacity to see that a road to Mashonaland running north and south had the disadvantage of crossing all the rivers, which flowed eastward to the sea. It was an even lesser tax on common sense to observe that while the South African ports—whence all supplies from outside Africa must come—were nearly two thousand miles from Salisbury, the sea coast to the east was only four or five hundred miles away. These truths had dawned almost simultaneously on Jameson and Johnson while they watched the pioneers dragging their wagons through fords and drifts which would become impassable torrents when the rains broke. Johnson's flights of imagination went even farther. He dreamed of a service of river steamers cruising serenely up the Pungwe, leaving a mere two or three hundred miles overland journey. The contract to deliver the column promised to leave him with a handsome little profit which would be crying out for reinvestment. As soon as he got to Salisbury he determined to survey this inviting route to the sea.

Jameson's little adventure eastward, when he had left the column with Selous at Fort Charter to look for the native chief of Manicaland, had been short-lived. One morning, in a flush of boyish effervescence, to win a bet from his companion, he had put his horse to jump a fallen tree, but the horse, having no personal interest in the wager, had refused and thrown him. The horse had been christened Lo Ben, a name which he lived up to by being generally hard-mouthed and obstinate. It was this horse which, some years later during the Matabele war, bolted with an officer straight into the Matabele lines where they were both promptly killed. The damage to Jameson was no worse than a couple of broken ribs, but he had to be carried back to Fort Charter—a three days' journey—on an improvised stretcher made by sticks and borne by unhandy natives, and the process was far from comfortable or painless. In due course he arrived in Salisbury, held rigid in a coat of plaster. Hearing that Johnson was off to find the sea, he insisted in joining him in the search.

With the column on its journey north to Salisbury had come another civilian, a Mr. Colquhoun. At the time, this gentleman's chief claim to fame had been when, as a distinguished pillar of the Indian Civil Service, he had sought to enlarge his income by acting clandestinely as correspondent of a London newspaper. That in itself had not caused embarrassment, but on one occasion he had been careless enough to misdirect his mail, and an official dispatch had gone to the paper's editor, while a journalistic effusion in his own handwriting, severely criticizing the administration of which he was a trusted servant, had found its way unerringly to the India Office.

The lapse had appealed to Rhodes, whose strange sense of values had no time for officialdom, and as Mr. Colquhoun was now looking for a job, Rhodes appointed him Administrator, or virtual dictator, of the Company's affairs in Mashonaland. In a country governed under royal charter, this meant he made the laws and enforced them. When he heard that Jameson and Johnson were planning an irresponsible excursion to the coast, through the worst lion and malaria infected region of southern Africa, he exerted his newly acquired authority and summarily forbade it.

The veto had no noticeable effect on the preparations for the journey. Johnson had carried with him, over the whole two thousand miles from the Cape, a collapsible boat. He had bought it in Cape Town from a certain Major Baden Powell who had no doubt adjured that on an overland journey one should at least be prepared. It was a formidable craft fully fourteen feet long, made in three sections each with a double bottom. The theory was that even if completely swamped the boat could not sink.

There were two distinguished sailors in Salisbury, Lieutenant Tyndale-Biscoe and one "Skipper" Hoste—who had been a captain in the old Union Steamship Line, forerunner of the Union Castle. Bringing their great experience to bear, they assembled the boat although there was no water to float it on. At the prodigal expense of a bottle of champagne, the craft was duly christened *Pioneer*. The ceremony having been completed in a sailor-like manner, the sections were dismounted and packed, with other supplies for the journey, in a wagon which was sent ahead into the empty veld with no more specific directions than to travel east.

The first dinner ever to be given in Salisbury was held as a farewell to Jameson and Johnson and their chosen companion, one Trooper Hay. Whether or not the Administrator attended the dinner is not known. Most likely he did not, for it is on record that the occasion was convivial, the general opinion being that the three travellers would never be seen again. The celebrations fittingly continued through the night and, in the early hours of an October morning in 1890, the guests rode out with Jameson, Johnson and Hay in an ambitious attempt to see them on the right road. As soon as the escort dropped out of sight, the intrepid expedition retired into the bush and went to sleep. Later in the day, as they painfully prepared to resume their journey into the unknown, they were accosted by a trooper of the Company's police who informed them, rather diffidently, that he had been sent by the Administrator to arrest them.

Jameson said, "Colquhoun! Damn the fellow! Go

back and tell him I got him his job." There is no record of how the Administrator received this piece of gratuitous information, but the expedition continued on its way without further hindrance.

Hay promised to be an asset to the party. He was a South African farmer, from Queenstown in the Cape. He was a good shot and spoke Kaffir well. Jameson, despite the apprenticeship of his long trips between Kimberley and Bulawayo, was still very raw and his plastered ribs were no advantage on a tough journey. Johnson says, "He was essentially a townsman. His best friend couldn't pretend that Providence had intended him for life in the open veld."

They took six horses and a Zulu boy, Jack, and they found their way by the simple expedient of following the tracks of the wagon that had been sent on ahead towards the sea. They had made no precise arrangement about where they would meet the wagon. About a hundred and fifty miles from Salisbury they came to the Penhalonga mountains and there, among the foothills, surprisingly enough, they found it.

They found too, here in the depth of the continent, an Englishman mining gold. He had been out of touch with the outside world for some time and had heard nothing of the occupation of Mashonaland. He showed understandable surprise when a party of white men rode out of the bush, and frank disbelief when they said they had come all the way overland from Cape Town. His name was Moodie and he was to fall so deeply under the spell of Jameson's magnetism that only three months later he was to set off with him on yet another improbable journey.

Now, he proved a great blessing to the expedition in search of the sea. The Penhalonga mountains formed an impassable barrier for the wagon with its stores and the indispensable boat, and it was unloaded and sent back to Salisbury. Nobody without influence could have hoped to convert the local natives into a team of willing carriers. Moodie collected thirty carriers—four were needed merely for each section of the boat—and at his forceful instigation they struggled unenthusiastically over the tortuous mountain tracks, encouraged only by the promise of a length of calico as reward at the other end. The white men, and their privileged Zulu servant, followed on horses as comfortably as conditions allowed.

In that district which lies on what is to-day the border between Rhodesia and Portuguese East Africa, there dwelt in the primitive splendour of the Macequece fort a Portuguese nobleman, Baron Rezende, who was the representative of the Mozambique Company. The fort, which had been built of mud many years before, looked imposing enough but was on the verge of crumbling away.

The Mozambique Company had long enjoyed a Charter from the King of Portugal giving it the same monopolistic rights in this part of the country as the Queen of England had more recently granted in the same territory exclusively to the British South Africa Company. Despite this remarkable coincidence and its awkward implications, Jameson and Johnson felt it their duty to pay the Baron a courtesy visit. Their motives might have included the possibility of a night under a roof and a bath, although they were not too sure that this last amenity could reasonably be expected of a Portuguese outpost.

They were received with frigid diplomatic politeness and when, as a matter of form, they asked the Baron's consent to their journey through what he was pleased to consider his own territory, he gave it only grudgingly. Nor did his hospitality extend to the offer of a cup of tea. As they had ridden some distance from their camp to make the call, and there was no chance of getting back before darkness fell, and they had brought no blankets, they spent a cheerless night outside the disintegrating walls of the fort. When they rejoined their party the next morning, they made a wide detour in case after all the Baron had changed his mind.

Up in the mountains, at Chimoio, they met another high-ranking Portuguese official, Colonel Machado. When he saw the party's horses he was too awed to be anything but friendly. He knew of the belt of country between Chimoio and the sea where the tsetse fly spelt certain death to horses. To have suggested the animals could have come from the other direction would have meant that they had been ridden all the way from the Cape, and *that* the Colonel could not believe. Jameson said nothing to disturb his wonder at their immunity from horse sickness, and sold them to him for a respectable sum. Then the whole party plunged on foot into a dense bamboo forest which took them three days to pass through. Emerging at last, they found the Pungwe river.

At this point of its course the Pungwe showed little promise of bearing a fleet of steamers on its bosom. It was wide enough from bank to bank, but its actual channel could be seen twisting uncertainly round sandbanks and over boulders, alternating between pools in which huge hippos comfortably submerged themselves, and shallows but a few inches deep.

The party assembled the boat and found it incapable of accommodating four men. The little matter of its possible capacity had been overlooked by the marine experts in Salisbury. When Jameson, Johnson and Hay sat in it, there were but a few inches of freeboard left and when the burly Zulu Jack stepped on board its unsinkable qualities forsook the craft and it promptly submerged. Jack, who was the only one of the party with a definite object to his journey—the white men had airily offered to carry him somehow down the coast to his home in Zululand, a thousand miles south—had to be left behind on the inhospitable banks of the Pungwe. He faced a lonely walk on the journey of two hundred miles back to Salisbury. But back to Salisbury and his masters he went and later, in the Matabele war, he fought for them and was killed.

Progress down the upper reaches of the river was slow, as the boat had to be dragged almost as far as it floated. The first evening they came fortuitously to the Portuguese city of Sarmento, which consisted of half a hundred grass houses set in a clearing on the river bank.

The party was welcomed effusively by the resident magistrate who boasted the high-sounding title of Intendente and whom Johnson describes as a seemingly much-married half-caste. In the name of Portugal he offered the travellers the hospitality of his guest house, a grass hut next to his own at the eastern end of the city. Fortunately there was no furniture taking up unnecessary space in the house so there was just room for the three of them to lie flat on the floor. They brought the sail of the boat up from the river to cover the bare earth. They brought up all their other possessions from the boat too and, where possible, crowded them into the house, mistakenly believing they would be safer out of reach of the city's inhabitants. All they left outside were the oars and the boat's mast, because these were too big to bring in.

Their clothes and boots were wet from almost constant immersion during their day's journey down the river. They hung everything up to dry under the roof of the house—again under the illusion that this was the safest place—and lay down to take their ease in the abbreviated drapery of their singlets. Hay, called by nature, put on his boots and went outside.

Like all great explorers, Jameson kept a diary. He stuck a candle in a bottle and set to work recording, for the undeserving benefit of posterity, how his party had braved the upper reaches of the Pungwe. Pleased with a particularly happy turn of phrase he called Johnson over to read and savour it. Johnson stumbled over the bottle and the candle fell against the grass wall of the house. The two

men, arrayed modestly in their singlets, just had time to
scramble outside, salvaging what little they could, before
the house went up in a sheet of flame.

A series of sharp explosions followed immediately, as
their precious cartridges went off one by one. The explosions were fortunate as they served to warn the inhabitants
of the city that something unusual was afoot, and tragedy
was averted because everyone turned out of their houses
to see what was going on.

The Intendente's and the guest house were at the eastern
end of the city and as the wind was blowing from that
direction—as it usually does in that part of Africa—the fire
soon spread and in a matter of minutes the city of Sarmento
ceased to exist. Only the Intendente's house was spared,
because it was up-wind from the fire, which happy circum-
stance mollified his feelings and disposed him more favourably towards the now half-naked visitors when the rest of
the population started showing signs of unmistakable
disapprobation.

In the split-second urgency of the moment, Johnson had
had the presence of mind to grab a rifle. He was wearing
next his skin, bulging under his singlet like a misshapen
brassière, a bandolier containing a score of cartridges and
nearly a hundred golden sovereigns. Remembering too
that—particularly in Portuguese territory—money won as
much respect as arms, he had also snatched up his writing
case in which were another couple of hundred pounds
worth of bank notes. But the cheap clasp of the case was
not designed for any sort of emergency and the bank notes,
and all the other interesting documents the case contained,
flew into the flames as surely as if they had been
thrown.

The only other salvage they mustered between them was
one dress slipper—the purpose of its inclusion in the
equipment of the expedition remains an interesting enigma
—a tin of icing sugar, a revolver without any cartridges

and a half-burnt photograph of Johnson's wife. Hay, whose call had come at a fortunate moment, enjoyed the luxury of a pair of boots. Down at the river there was still the boat and, lying outside the burnt-out house, out of reach of the fire, were the oars and the mast.

Beyond these opportune possessions the expedition had nothing but what it stood up in—although the phrase hardly describes the functions of a singlet. In these barely affluent circumstances they still had to travel another hundred and fifty miles to the coast and from there make their way back to civilization, a thousand miles or more away, by some route and means not yet determined.

The inhabitants of Sarmento were, not unnaturally, more concerned with their own predicament. Johnson reports that as night wore on there were, among the citizens, growing signs of peevishness as the theory spread among them that the three white men were responsible for the destruction of their city.

Johnson rose to the occasion in the best empire-building manner. He took out from his bandolier twenty shining sovereigns—nicely assessing the value of the damage—and, in the light of the glowing ruins of the city, presented them to the Intendente with an imperious gesture that was in no way diminished by his singlet's stark inability to conceal the manly endowments nature had bestowed upon him.

In an instant, the people were appeased. The Intendente invited the three white men to his own house and history is silent where he and his wives—and for that matter, the rest of the population—spent the remainder of the night.

Early next morning the travellers took once more to their boat, fortified with the blessing of the Intendente on behalf of his people, although there was an unseemly incident on the river bank when a few natives, who had not heard of the lavish restitution already made, were only restrained from doing violence by the deft stroke of an oar administered by Hay.

The journey that day hardly came up to Johnson's visions of a serene cruise down the river. With no protection from the sun, either on their heads or below their waists, they suffered considerably. Johnson and Hay had spent so long in the veld that the inconvenience was not too serious, but Jameson's raw city skin suffered painfully and rowing had an even more agonizing effect on his plastered ribs than riding.

They were in the wider reaches of the river now and it split into so many channels and they had so little knowledge of its navigation that all they could do was to row down it in the general expectation that in the end they would come to the sea. At night they tied themselves to what they thought was an island, hoping there to be immune from attack from wild beasts. It turned out that they had chosen the mainland in the most lion-infested district in the continent of Africa. Jameson said they could always re-live the experience of that night—if they were lunatic enough to wish to do so—by sitting out in singlets under a tree, by a smoking fire, in the moonlight on the patch of ground at the end of the old bear terraces at the London Zoo, and arranging for all the animals to be let out under the impression that a meal was waiting. The only feature that would be missing would be the mosquitoes, without which the night, under those circumstances, would be comparatively pleasant.

They rowed spasmodically through five days and one night, tying up to shelter from the sun or to snatch some sleep, in backwaters where hippos lunged and crocodiles cruised, waiting as hopefully for a meal as the travellers themselves. Johnson shot a buffalo and one duck, and nothing else. He had few cartridges and some of these had to be expended on a hunter's trick to make a fire, for all their matches had gone to help burn down Sarmento.

Twice they met the river bore, a tidal wave three feet high that on one occasion caught them with the boat partly dismantled as they were dragging it in sections over some shallows. The theory that the boat could not sink was, on these occasions, severely tested, and the icing-sugar tin used as a bailer proved more effective than the boat's double bottom.

On the fifth day, late in the afternoon, they found what they had been looking for—the sea. It came to meet them unmistakably in the estuary of the river.

Before they left Salisbury, Johnson had sent a casual letter to a friend in Cape Town asking him to arrange for a steamer to sail up the east coast of Africa to look for them. The letter had to be carried five hundred miles over the pioneer route before it reached the first of Her Majesty's Post Offices. Moreover the rains were likely to start any day, when the route would be impassable. Then there was the further hazard that Johnson's friend might be away from Cape Town. In the unlikely event of the letter reaching him, he was asked to send a ship to cruise between the most southern mouth of the Zambesi and Chiloane Island —along a mere hundred and fifty miles of African coast. With commendable forethought Johnson told him to instruct the skipper to look out for a flag by day or a bonfire by night. Being unable to bring the ship nearer than ten miles from the shore owing to hazards, the skipper's search for a solitary flag—which could only have been a singlet—along a hundred and fifty miles of heavily forested coast, turned out to be a little exacting. A fire at night was not so difficult to spot. Being the season for bush fires, there was one burning every few miles.

Johnson had mentioned no date for his probable arrival at an unspecified point on the coast. Otherwise the arrangements were admirable. The ship cruised painstakingly up and down the coast for twenty-nine days—at the expense of the Chartered Company which was always hard-pressed financially—and had put in to the mouths of the Busi and Pungwe rivers once a week.

That the afternoon when the river party met the sea happened to be one of the few occasions when the ship entered the Pungwe was no less than miraculous. With nice consideration for the Company's interests, the skipper had decided to give up the search altogether that afternoon but, having gone ashore, had shot a zebra and he waited overnight to collect the meat next morning.

The sun was about to go down, and the boat party was beginning to battle against the rising choppiness of the water, when Johnson saw two sticks standing up on the horizon which might be the masts of a ship. The river bank, which they were hugging tenaciously, swung away to the north and the ship if such it were was at least ten miles away hull down over the south-eastern horizon. His companions had less faith than Johnson that a ship of any sort, let alone one that might be looking for them, was ever likely to materialize along that part of the coast, and they showed no enthusiasm for attempting to cross an open reach of choppy sea in a collapsible boat in pursuit of a mirage.

Darkness fell, and the mirage surprisingly lit a riding light at her masthead. Even though she appeared to be out in the middle of the Indian Ocean she was obviously at anchor. The light was certainly no figment of the imagination, so a greater unanimity of decision prevailed in the boat and, risking the perils of an ocean voyage, they set their course for it, bow on to a rising sea.

The skipper of the steamer was a Scot. When he found that the light had been hoisted while the ship rode at anchor miles away from the likely track of any other steamers, the thought of such reckless expenditure of oil shocked him and he providently ordered the light to be extinguished.

When the light went out the crew of the *Pioneer* had nothing left to steer by, so they tried to turn back to the shore. But the sea was now too heavy to allow them to do anything but keep bow on to the waves, unless the unsinkable boat were to be swamped and founder with all hands. So they had no option but to keep on rowing out into the Indian Ocean. The only comforting knowledge was that the strong ebb tide which was taking them out to sea would at some time turn, when they might have a faint chance of struggling back to land.

But Fate had ordained that Jameson was not to be drowned in the unfriendly waters of the Pungwe, nor to be marooned in a singlet without supplies and left either to starve or die of malaria on the fever-ridden coast of Portuguese East Africa. For it was certainly no skill or judgment, and least of all forethought, that carried the slowly sinking *Pioneer*, with her fraudulent double bottom, on such a course that she virtually rammed in the dark the ship that had been sent to find her on the long and ill-charted east coast of Africa.

Nor was that the only miracle. The steamer, *Lady Wood*, secure in the knowledge that there could be no other vessels within a hundred miles, carried no watch on deck, and the tide that had carried the *Pioneer* bearing down on her would just as readily have swept the little boat past her and out to sea. By a chance in a million, someone on the ship came on deck as the boat bumped alongside and the men in her shouted despairingly. That they did find the ship, and were heard, and in the end were taken aboard, no doubt justified in his own mind the skipper's thoughtfulness in economizing in lamp oil.

Thus was pioneered the route from Salisbury to the sea. Beyond proving that the sea was where they expected it to be, the members of the expedition effected little of practical value. Not that such a consideration should ever detract from the pure milk of exploration.

Jameson, Johnson and Hay, in their attenuated singlets, braved the perils of travel through the unknown as surely as Scott and Amundsen, without all the fuss and prolonged preparations usually associated with trips to the Poles. Fortunately for them, when reduced to singlets, they had to contend with heat and not frost.

They had ridden over two hundred miles on their horses, walked another fifty and, clad only in their faith, had rowed and dragged their boat yet another hundred and fifty over the scarcely navigable reaches of the Pungwe. Fate had a lot in store for Jameson and that, if nothing else, had guided them to safety.

VIII

T HE Portuguese had been in Africa for three hundred
years and showed every sign of having come to stay.
They had first come in the great days when world
discovery was fashionable and Portugal in those times had
been one of the leaders of the fashion. Those were the
heroic days when men dressed themselves for their jobs
regardless of climate. The intrepid Francesco Barreto
would never have set out in a singlet. It was back in the
sixteenth century that he had landed near the mouth of
the Zambesi and marched inland in search of Monomopata,
his men and heroes splendidly arrayed in full armour flash-
ing in the grilling sun. The great sheets of iron mail
became so hot they were unbearable to touch and beneath
them the warriors virtually roasted alive. Like a lot of
other people, Barreto never found Monomopata but he
found a very uncomfortable death.

Since Barreto's failure to carry Africa with his flaming
sword, the Portuguese had shown little enthusiasm for leaving the vineyards of Europe and settling in their new
colony. The early pioneers who did settle on the coast
performed most of their colonization by the agreeable practice of local dissemination, and by the nineteenth century
there was a creditable half-caste population dotted about all
over Portuguese East Africa.

By then, there were many African natives there too.
These were mainly Shangaans, a tribe that had broken away
from the Zulus as the Matabele had done, and at about
the same time. Their northward saga had not been as

90

picturesque as that of the Matabele, but it had had its fair share of bloodshed and rapine. So, unlike the other quietly settled tribes in that part of the world, the Shangaans with their Zulu ancestry were a fair match for the Matabele and enjoyed a real independence.

They were ruled by a chief with the exuberant name of Gungunyana, who called himself King of Gazaland. He was reputed to have sworn allegiance to the King of Portugal, but if he did, he probably had no idea what it was all about. His kraal, Manhlagazi, stood a few miles north of the banks of the Limpopo, right down in the south-eastern corner of the territory. It was an unhealthy fever-ridden spot and the mortality among his people was high but, like so many Africans throughout the centuries, they had no option but to be content with their fate.

There was another chief of some prominence in the land, Chief Umtasa, and he ruled a tribe known as the Manicas, who dwelt some hundreds of miles north of Gungunyana's kraal, in the area between Salisbury and the sea. Umtasa himself was not so susceptible to fever because he lived on the top of a mountain and had a strong addiction to alcohol.

Both Gungunyana and the Portuguese claimed him as their vassal, but he enjoyed a sense of self-sufficiency that was not wholly due to the altitude of his kraal, and he disdainfully repudiated the claims of both. He might have done worse than to cast his fortunes with the Portuguese, for they still had influence in Europe strong enough to discourage outside interference, and for the last two hundred years they had shown they were quite happy to leave the natives to go their own way and that the only claims they had on them were pleasantly progenitive. They cast less envious eyes on their land than on their women, in happy contrast to the other white men now coming to Africa, who were greedy for land and showed generally an aversion to black women. Also, the Portuguese put a rationally large part of their efforts into making wine, which bound Umtasa to them with a happy link.

When Jameson had left the pioneer column at Fort Charter with Selous, his intention had been to beard Umtasa in his kraal. He had every hope of wringing a couple of concessions out of the chief, painfully, as they had been wrung out of Lobengula. Once more he would sit for months at the stubborn feet of a black king and argue. Colquhoun, the Administrator designate, the only other civilian with the column—who, like Selous, was not regarded by Major Johnson as an asset to the expedition—had come with the party. When Jameson had fallen ingloriously from his horse, Colquhoun and Selous had taken over the task.

Travelling towards the sunrise they left the column behind them, and they left behind too the wide plains of bleached grass and entered a furrowed world of blue mountains and lush green valleys. Selous, who knew the country well, led Colquhoun straight to the chief's kraal perched at the top of his rocky crag.

Colquhoun extracted a concession from Umtasa within a couple of weeks, almost before the column had had time to reach Salisbury. It was a suspiciously easy diplomatic victory. Without a quibble, Umtasa gave him the mineral rights in Manicaland and an undertaking not to give anyone else any land, in return for a specious promise of British protection from the inoffensive Portuguese, and the inevitable hundred pounds. Umtasa agreed, too, with remarkable alacrity, to the appointment of a British Resident in the sanctuary of his kraal, and a British police force for Manicaland. He said, in effect, walk in, my friends, and take the country from me. It was unlikely that he was entirely sober at the time, but he knew well enough—even better than Lobengula had known—what he had done.

To Colquhoun, who was used to the unchallenged power of the British Raj over Indian natives, the easy success of his mission was but a matter of course. Arrived in Salisbury before the column had even been disbanded, he blandly told Jameson that all the fuss about negotiating with African chiefs was grossly exaggerated. All that was needed was experience. Here was proof in the ready way Umtasa had accepted his terms. Jameson said nothing at the time, even forbearing to comment on the circumstances of the other's appointment, but the seeds of a strong antagonism had been sown.

Of course, Umtasa's acceptance of the terms in no way implied that he intended to honour them. He had understood them perfectly but, like all African chiefs, he reserved to himself the right to say afterwards he had not. This could always be relied on as a sure bait for sympathy from people outside Africa. He understood them so well that within a few hours one of his messengers was at Macequece fort, telling Baron Rezende that the British had imposed their demands on him by a shocking threat of force.

Baron Rezende, when he learned that the British were after exactly what the Portuguese had for many years presumed to be theirs already, upheld Umtasa's plaint that no one had any right to make such demands on him. He promised to come over as soon as he could to put matters in their proper light. It was while these exchanges were taking place that Jameson and Johnson, on their way to the sea, had innocently paid their call at Macequece fort, and so the embargo on a cup of tea was perhaps understandable.

Although the Portuguese had done little effective colonization, there were plenty of high-ranking officials in the country. In addition to the Baron, who was a director of the Mozambique Company, the district—known as the Gorongoza Province—boasted a Principal Agent of the Company, Colonel d'Andrade, and a Military Governor, Manuel Antonio de Souza.

D'Andrade held the military rank and de Souza ran the army. In the local tradition, de Souza was a half-caste.

Despite the adequate choice available from his own names, he was known locally as Gouveia. Following the estimable practice of his forbears, he consorted unaffectedly with native women. Some of them he even married, thus ensuring military support from their tribes. As Military Governor he was well placed to monopolize the trade of the province, with slavery as a profitable sideline, and the supply of young girls for his harem assured. For these invaluable services to his country, the Portuguese government paid him handsomely and saw that he was well supplied with arms.

Learning the threat to Umtasa, the three eminent officials —the Baron, the Colonel and the Military Governor— hurried to his kraal with earnest assurances that they had only come to look after his interests. When Umtasa saw that Gouveia had brought with him a couple of hundred troops he was not so sure, and he sent a plaintive call to Salisbury for British protection from the Portuguese according to the terms of the concession. Things were working out as he planned. All he now had to do was to sit back with a bottle and watch the Portuguese and British get at each other's throats on the treacherously steep slopes of his kraal. They would both roll down to their deaths in the deep valley below and leave him to drink in peace.

Colquhoun sent a force of police from Salisbury which, if not in overwhelming strength, was at least adequately officered. It consisted of ten troopers, four civilians with nothing better to do, attracted by the prospect of action with an army to which they did not belong, and three officers—Captain Forbes, who commanded, and two lieutenants. There was also Mr. Doyle, an interpreter, and a press correspondent, Beauman, who became the only casualty of the expedition, being taken unceremoniously by a lion when, on the march one afternoon, he slipped modestly into the bush to answer a call by nature. The only trace left of him were his boots, with his feet still in them.

When the force, seventeen strong, arrived at the foot of Umtasa's kraal and learned from their intelligence reports that there were at least a hundred and fifty armed natives with Gouveia, they wisely went into hiding and sent a runner to the nearest police post at Fort Charter for reinforcements. While they were waiting, the Navy—ubiquitous as ever—in the shape of Lieutenant Tyndale-Biscoe and "Skipper" Hoste, arrived with despatches. With them was Regimental Sergeant-Major King, so the supernumerary ranks of the army were suitably strengthened. Even so, the fighting strength still remained at ten, with four irregulars.

At last, from Fort Charter, came Lieutenant the Honourable Eustace Fiennes with fifteen troopers, so Forbes felt himself adequately strong to join action. Forbes had been seconded to the B.S.A. Police from the Inniskilling Dragoons, so there could be no doubt of his qualifications as a soldier. Johnson, who was sometimes apt to be a little carping, described him as a typical British bulldog, with as much sense. Forbes sent his men up the mountain to attack the kraal from the rear and perhaps it was his military intuition that told him that Gouveia had not alerted any troops nor posted any sentries. In any case, his guess was right, which was fortunate.

There had been an impressive little ceremony at the kraal during the afternoon. D'Andrade had summoned all the European settlers in the district to hear from Umtasa's own lips to whom the country really belonged. With Gouveia's troops in the background it was a calculated risk. Umtasa cast his bloodshot eyes over the western horizon, but there were no signs of the British protection for which he had given away the concession—which part of the arrangements he had somehow never mentioned to the Portuguese.

The protection now seemed to have turned out to be no more than a fraudulent promise, while the presence of Gouveia's braves with their rusty rifles was an awkward reality. Without the power to protest, Umtasa suffered a Portuguese flag to be run up the pole in the centre of the kraal and reluctantly acknowledged Portuguese sovereignty over his land and his people. Then, determined to extract some benefit from an unhappy occasion, he invited the Portuguese notables into his hut to join him in drinking to his own unshakable loyalty.

While the enemy were thus agreeably engaged, Forbes and his men, panting a little from the climb, walked through a gap in the stockade surrounding the kraal and a trooper was sent to run down the flag and substitute a Union Jack. The open space in front of the chief's hut was crowded with natives and they fell back in some excitement and confusion from the armed strangers. The noise brought the three Portuguese officials to the door of the hut and, without undue ceremony, Captain Forbes proceeded summarily to take them prisoners—three nationals of a country with whom Britain was not even remotely at war, and in a territory over which she had no valid authority to rule.

Forbes charged them with "intriguing and conspiring with natives in a British territory", an offence which it would have been difficult to find prescribed in any statute book. D'Andrade and Gouveia protested against their arrest with hearty Latin vehemence, but the Baron preserved an aristocratic dignity. The crowd, having so recently heard their chief's declaration of loyalty to the men who were now captive before them, were not a little confused about their own position. Umtasa himself set their minds at rest by staggering to the door and inviting Forbes and his men into the hut to drink to his unwavering loyalty to the British crown. Forbes refused ungraciously and, in the view of his companions, mistakenly, for it was a hot afternoon and the sun was on the point of going down.

Colonel d'Andrade and the Military Governor of Gorogonza Province were marched to Salisbury under close arrest. Baron Rezende was sent back to the fort at Macequece, possibly on the grounds that that would be sufficient punishment. From Salisbury, d'Andrade and Gouveia were passed along, with other packages in transit, down the pioneer road to the south. On the way down, they met Dr. Jameson, travelling up country again after his trip to the coast. Observing the social demands of the occasion, in the middle of empty Africa, d'Andrade cut him. Gouveia, who had not been so well brought up, burst into tears and pleaded for release. However, he was soon able to dry his tears for, at Kimberley, the Governor-General's train was waiting for the prisoners.

The arrests had not been so easy to justify in the more ordered civilization south of the Limpopo. It was not the last time the Cape Government would have to make amends for the indiscretions of its Prime Minister, for there is no doubt that Rhodes was fully aware of what his people were up to in Manicaland. So every effort was made to mollify the erstwhile prisoners and they were sent back to Portugal, first-class, at the Company's expense. Much of their previous indignity was atoned when the British flagship at Simonstown fired a salute in their honour.

The orders given to Forbes when he was sent off with ten men had been to occupy as much of the country as possible. He proposed to interpret these orders liberally, particularly as his effective strength had been doubled and, leaving three men to occupy Manicaland—a mere ten thousand square miles—he set off in Jameson's wake towards the sea.

The first obstacle was the Macequece fort but, as the Military Governor of the district had been wafted away, the garrison had seized the opportunity and gone off home and the mortified Baron was in sole occupation. The outpost of

Portugal surrendered without a fight. The Navy took over and, prodigally supported by four more men, remained to subjugate the district. At Chimoio's kraal, where Jameson had so satisfactorily disposed of his horses, two more men were left to maintain the line of communication. The rest of the army pressed forward on the long march to Beira. One after another the far-flung strongholds of Portugal surrendered ignominiously to the invaders.

But the arrival in the Cape of two inoffensive Portuguese officials under close arrest had stirred dangerous international currents. Panic despatches were telegraphed from Cape Town to Mafeking and pressed on by relays of horsemen through Forts Tuli, Victoria and Charter to Salisbury, ordering the immediate withdrawal of the invading hordes from Manicaland.

Colquhoun, who had always doubted the wisdom of these adventures to the east, looked round hastily for someone to be sent to recall Forbes. Jameson's friends showed a suspicious concern over this search for a suitable messenger. Before Colquhoun could suggest anyone else, they presented their man to him with glowing recommendations and, at their urgent insistence, he was sent off in the vague direction of the coast. As he had never been known to find his way in the bush, and as he now had no maps, it was a comforting certainty he would lose himself, and Forbes would reach Beira unhindered.

Unfortunately for Rhodesia which, sixty years later, is still without a port, the hapless messenger chose this occasion to find his way without difficulty. Inordinately proud of himself, he presented his orders to Forbes to retire. Forbes was a soldier and had never got anybody a job, so he had no option but to obey. The lines of communication were rolled up, the army withdrew, and the Macequece fort was restored to the affronted Baron. Ill-feeling rankled among all parties except Umtasa who had commuted his hundred pounds for a virtually unlimited supply of cheap

Portuguese brandy, and was now to be left in peace to enjoy the fruits of his shrewd transaction.

But the true honour of Portugal was not to be so easily vindicated. A wave of righteous indignation swept through Lisbon when they heard there-of the shocking indignities to their great empire-builders. These had been insults that a great Latin race could only wipe out in blood and, early in 1891, a volunteer army of five hundred young men sailed down the Tagus, bound for Africa but destined for little glory.

This army of liberation landed at Beira at the end of February, at the height of the rainy season when the mosquitoes were at the top of their form. Entirely without training, these amateur soldiers would have fallen out on a route march of any length, even in the temperate fields of Europe. On the banks of the Pungwe they merely laid down and died, and when the remains of the fever-stricken army struggled into Macequece fort two months after it had marched off from Beira, there were less than a hundred of her youth left to avenge Portugal's tarnished honour.

In a well-intentioned effort to avoid further unpleasantness, the governments of Portugal and the United Kingdom had agreed to an arbitrary division of Manicaland into what they were pleased to call their respective spheres of influence. The fort at Macequece was still to stand as Portugal's crumbling outpost on the east of the new dividing line. On its west would be the Chartered Company's new township of Umtali, near Umtasa's kraal. Situated as they were on an explosive frontier—despite what the governments in Europe might choose to believe—the citizens of the little town felt the need of an adequate garrison, and at their insistent request Colquhoun sent a Captain Heyman with no less than thirty men.

When the news reached Heyman that the remnants of the army of the Tagus had staggered into Macequece fort, he sent a peremptory demand for an explanation of this wanton act of provocation. The high offices in Portuguese East Africa had, of necessity, been redistributed, and now a Colonel Ferreira boasted the hopeful title of Governor of Manica. He had never had a hundred Europeans in his army before and, with a force of such limitless possibilities at his disposal, he saw fit to reply to Heyman that his men were there to drive all the English out of the country.

Such a provocation would delight the heart of any soldier and Heyman, carefully avoiding any possible mischance of receiving guidance from his superiors at Salisbury, advanced with his own army of thirty to Chua Hill, overlooking Macequece. His ranks were stiffened by fifteen irregulars who found life in Umtali uninspiring and had no intention of missing a war on their doorstep. Apart from a seven-pounder gun, the army lacked equipment, and all the horses were down with horse sickness although this turned out to be an advantage as they would have been a handicap on the waterless crags of Chua Hill.

Heyman had no intention of repeating the risk Forbes had taken at Umtasa's kraal. This time he would make sure that it was the enemy who fought uphill. He marched his army to the top of the kopje—well over the new frontier —and placed a few men provocatively in full view of the fort. He allowed only a dozen or so to be seen against the skyline, where they could be easily counted. He had no intention of showing any more, as a superiority of less than eight to one might well discourage the Portuguese from attacking. He emphasized his weakness by sending a signaller to stand on a boulder at the top of the hill—well beyond the range of any Portuguese marksman—semaphoring desperately into the western distance for reinforcements.

Now the provocation had rebounded, and this time it was the surviving flower of Portuguese youth who found it more than they could stand. Here in front of them was the enemy they had come five thousand uncomfortable miles to fight, in gratifying weakness and obviously uneasy.

Over the horizon there might be a big army approaching—perhaps as many as fifty men—for more signallers had been sent up on to the skyline and the flags were waving so wildly as to be incoherent. The Portuguese had three hundred native levies to go into battle with them, consequently the outcome of the fight could not be in doubt. It never was —for that very reason.

There was nothing glorious about the victory Captain Heyman and his fifty odd men won that day. They merely had to wait comfortably behind the boulders on Chua Hill and pick out the wretched young Portuguese as they climbed the hill and came within easy range. The native troops fled after the first burst of rifle fire, leaving thirty dead.

News of the impending battle had gone out far and wide and the civilian native population from miles around had gathered expectantly in its hundreds on the slopes of the surrounding hills. In those days, war was properly confined to those immediately engaged and the spectators enjoyed the battle in perfect safety. When only the two white teams were left in the game, the crowd waited breathlessly to see which side it could henceforth support as its champions.

For two hours the young men from Lisbon gallantly contended against a hopeless situation, but at last they withdrew to the doubtful protection of the fort. Heyman prudently stayed at the top of the hill for the rest of the day, and next morning he advanced cautiously to find the fort deserted, and a handful of British police once more became masters of Manicaland.

The way to Beira lay open again, and this time Lieutenant Fiennes was sent forward, ostensibly to follow up the Portuguese retreat. Once more, an east coast port for Rhodesia was within grasp.

Unfortunately, Johnson had been giving glowing accounts in the Cape about the east coast route from Salisbury to the sea, as advance publicity for the profitable mail service he planned to operate over it. His propaganda had been so successful that two distinguished travellers, Bishop Knight Bruce and a Major Sapte, had essayed the journey in the opposite direction and, properly equipped—without any risk of being reduced to singlets—they travelled confidently westwards from the coast and met Fiennes and his punitive force hurrying east.

What the Bishop had to say about treatment of one's neighbours may not have had a marked effect on Fiennes' intentions. But Major Sapte was military secretary to none less than the British High Commissioner in South Africa and he had come to settle once and for all the disputes with the Portuguese which were causing such embarrassment in Europe. Fiennes knew he had only to walk into Beira and hoist the Union Jack and the port would be British. In the august world where military secretaries dwelt, things were not as easily arranged as that, and with an alacrity of decision for a staff officer, as unfortunate as it was remarkable, he ordered Fiennes and the army back to Salisbury.

When, in time, Rhodes heard what had happened, he said angrily, " Why didn't Fiennes say Sapte was drunk, and put him in irons? "

Empire-building had never profited from scruples.

IX

WITH twenty thousand pounds of the Company's precious capital, Rhodes bought a handy little steamer in Port Elizabeth, the *Countess of Carnarvon*. In a more conventional business the directors might have wanted to know why a land-locked country needed an ocean-going steamship. Although Johnson had spoken grandly of cruises up the Pungwe, his experience of dragging a collapsible boat over the shallows had hardly served to sustain even his own enthusiasm for river transport. Nor could the directors really be expected to provide a standing patrol up the coast of Africa to pick up half-naked explorers with an urge to go looking for the sea.

Nevertheless, with commendable foresight, Rhodes had included among the objects of the Company, clearly set out in the Charter, the power to acquire, hold, charter and "otherwise deal with" steam vessels. It was not the sort of expressed object usually to be found in the memorandum of a company whose sphere of operations is to be at least five hundred miles from the sea, and whose biggest internal waterway is likely to be a farm dam. Yet out of a list of fifteen business-like and conventional objects laid down in the Charter of the British South Africa Company, the intention to operate a fleet of ships holds pride of second place, priority being given only to the unavoidable obligation to issue shares.

The promise of yet another concession, on the familiar lines, had been wheedled out of Gungunyana, the King of

Gazaland. Gazaland was as big as Matabeleland and Mashonaland put together, so the concession was priced at the standard figure of a thousand rifles and twenty thousand rounds of ammunition with, this time, the extra inducement of five hundred pounds a year. There was, too, this difference—that while Lobengula had been persuaded to sell his own country, Gungunyana was offering what the Portuguese thought was theirs, so he wisely insisted on payment in advance.

To land openly on the Portuguese coast and deliver arms to a native chief in what the Portuguese considered their own sovereign territory might have been a little inexpedient, and it was here that the provisions of the second clause of the Charter came in handy. Gungunyana's kraal was but fifty miles from the banks of the Limpopo, a river of very different calibre from the Pungwe. Respectable-sized steamers could navigate a hundred miles or more up the river and there was a landing stage at Chai Chai, the nearest point on the river to the King's kraal. The rifles and ammunition could be landed there, out of sight of the Portuguese authorities, and slipped in to Gungunyana by the back door.

A seaman with intimate knowledge of the channel, one Captain Buckingham, was put in command of the *Countess of Carnarvon*. The Captain put his heart and soul into his appointed task of gun-running, emboldened by the knowledge that he was under the orders of a Company with the respectability of Queen Victoria's charter.

The Portuguese navy had a gunboat on the coast, the *Maréchal Macmahon*—why the Portuguese should name one of their warships after a French marshal of Irish extraction, is irrelevant—and Captain Buckingham slyly waited until she ran up on the slips at Durban to have the barnacles scraped off her bottom, before he put to sea in the *Countess of Carnarvon* with his cargo of contraband. He had with him on board a Mr. Stevens, carrying five hundred of the

Company's brightest golden sovereigns, and a Captain Pawley with an armed detachment of the British South Africa Police.

Altogether, it was as piratical a little expedition as could be wished for. On the seventeenth of February 1891, shamelessly flying the Blue Ensign, it crossed the bar of the Limpopo, blandly ignoring the frantic signals to stop waved by the customs house which the Portuguese had established at the mouth of the river.

At Chai Chai, Captain Buckingham disembarked Stevens, Pawley and the police and dumped the cases of rifles and ammunition on the landing stage, in the full light of the African sun. Then, rather than suffer any possible interest on the part of the Portuguese, and the certain attentions of the mosquitoes, he sailed down the river and out to sea, promising to return and pick up the party in a week's time.

The Portuguese customs men soon covered the twenty miles along the river bank to the landing stage and had no difficulty in identifying the contents of the cases. Stevens had already hurried inland with the money, and Pawley found himself left to deal with the officials. Being a good policeman he always showed nice respect, if not for the law, at least for its guardians, so he suffered without demur the imposition of a fine of two thousand pounds for illegal importation—a penalty that was softened by the reassuring thought that he would not have to pay it himself.

He carried no money but, encouraged by the presence of his armed troopers, the Portuguese agreed to take his bond. They decided, too, that the cases were too heavy to confiscate and that as all the rifles were old and rusty they were hardly worth taking away. So, as soon as their backs were turned, Pawley and his men collected a gang of native carriers and humped the cases through the swampy veld to Gungunyana's kraal. The bond being thus broken, Rhodes was committed to another two thousand pounds as part of the price of an abortive concession—for Gazaland has remained Portuguese to this day.

At Gungunyana's kraal they found the ubiquitous Dr. Jameson, in his familiar state of ragged distress at the end of yet another epic overland journey. It was less than five months since, in October, he had first left Salisbury in search of the sea. During these few months, first, the *Lady Wood* had taken him on an unpleasantly rough trip to Port Elizabeth, whence he had travelled five hundred miles overland to Cape Town to tell Rhodes about the delights of the Pungwe, and, incidentally, to persuade him first to enter his own country by that route. Then he had covered once more the thousand miles over the pioneer route to Salisbury. He had arrived in Salisbury just in time to enjoy the first Rhodesian Christmas and, only three days later, had set off for Umtali, one hundred and fifty miles away, to see what all the fuss with the Portuguese was about.

At Umtali, the situation had got out of hand. There were no results to be shown from Colquhoun's vaunted concession and, except in Umtasa's opinion, the hundred pounds paid for it seemed to have been wasted.

Even so, Umtasa was complaining that, while his contemporaries were all being paid with arms for their lands, he had been fobbed off with a spurious promise of protection, and a few rolls of calico thrown in as a bonus. The calico was good for little else than to make dresses for his wives, and he could see no particular attraction in this urge to drape the female form—even though the best he could feast his eyes on were a few besotted old harridans lounging around his kraal.

Despite Colquhoun's enthusiasm for what he had accomplished with Umtasa, Jameson had believed all along that the key to Gazaland and Manicaland was with Gungunyana in his kraal, seven or eight hundred miles to the south. The concession from Umtasa had been worth no more than was paid for it, but one from Gungunyana could be worth a lot more than even the chief himself might be likely to ask. Jameson knew something of the negotiations that had already been started, and in Cape Town he had heard talk of the *Countess of Carnarvon* and her exciting possibilities. If there was to be any piracy in Africa, he had no intention of being out of it. So, undeterred by his experiences on the Pungwe, he set off once again with but two companions on an uncharted journey through the bush, over a route that no white man was likely ever to have travelled before.

He took as a companion Moodie, the English miner he and Johnson had met in the Penhalonga mountains on their previous trip. Jameson had been impressed with his practical knowledge of the country. In any event, however, it was not Moodie, the tough miner with long experience of Africa, who was to smooth the path for the city-bred little doctor, but Jameson who, by sheer powers of almost superhuman endurance, was to lead Moodie and the third member of the party back to the civilization that sometimes they must have despaired of ever seeing again.

The third man was Dennis Doyle, who had travelled with Jameson as his interpreter on the journeys to Lobengula at Bulawayo. He had been compound manager at the De Beers mine at Kimberley—a position carrying the same sort of unbridled authority as a prison governor. He was a fine linguist but was apt to let his imagination run away with him when interpreting. It was he who had conveyed to Lobengula the supposed message from Queen Victoria which Jameson had concocted from Whitehall's "unintelligible rubbish", and he had probably added his own telling embellishments. Even Lobengula saw through him on occasion, and once said, "All white men are liars," —it was a theme on which he dwelt—"and Doyle is the father of all liars."

Jameson, who often saw eye to eye with Lobengula, trusted Doyle but little and it was only because there was

no other interpreter available that he agreed to take him
to Gungunyana's kraal.

Before they started, Doyle insisted on Jameson's signing
an agreement that the Company would pay ten thousand
pounds to his widow if he died on the trip. Ten thousand
pounds of the Company's money was neither here nor there
to Jameson, and the idea of death in the wilds of Africa
seemed to him extravagant. When, a little later, Doyle
caught fever and showed every sign of succumbing, Jameson had some bad moments wondering whether the Company would honour the fat life insurance policy he had so
blithely underwritten on their behalf without giving them
a chance to lay off the risk. The possibility of their repudiation, leaving him to honour the debt himself, was the
strongest incentive to save a patient's life he had experienced
in his medical career.

As on the previous trip, the party started off fairly well
equipped for a journey through wild country. They had
two horses and a mule between them and twenty carriers
for their supplies. It was January and still the height of
the first rainy season—which men remembered for years as
one of the worst—and the rivers were swollen and almost
impassable. But they planned to cross all the rivers, except
the Sabi, at their headwaters and these were easy enough
to ford. Even so, after only a few days, one of the innocent-
looking streams on the high veld carried away the wretched
mule and most of their provisions, and once more Jameson
found himself in the middle of Africa with two companions,
a long journey before them, and little more than their
wits to keep them alive. The disaster was certainly nothing like the fire at Sarmento, but it was serious enough and
the uninviting outlook was more than the native carriers
could face. They knew Africa too well to hanker after what
adventures she had to offer. So the three white men were
left to carry what they could themselves, with only two
horses between them.

The journey took forty-seven days and, after they had crossed the Sabi—half a mile wide at its most fordable point—each day became a nightmare and the nights even worse. They were back in the low veld, at the worst season of the year. They dragged themselves through swamps and mud and, at one period, it rained unceasingly for eleven days.

The rain beat down in torrents, as it always does on the low veld, and the country was so flat there was no run-off of water. It was ideal for the mosquitoes, and all three men caught fever. Moodie was ill, but kept going. Doyle became desperately ill. Jameson himself ran a high temperature, but knew that if once they stopped they would never move on again. Splashing through swamps and squelching through mud, he supported Doyle on a horse and they dragged themselves painfully through the bush. At last, on February 28th, fever-ridden and bordering on collapse, they struggled up to the little plateau on which Gungunyana had built his city.

At the first hut they came to on the outskirts of the city a native was arguing fiercely with a young lady who had no false modesty about her attire. With some difficulty, they interrupted the discussion and asked the man for food and water. Grasping the heaven-sent opportunity to be able to meet the price the lady was holding out for, he offered what they wanted at an extortionate rate of barter.

The red corpuscles of Jameson's blood may have suffered at the hands of the malaria germ, but its Scots quality was unimpaired and he showed no hesitation in refusing the offer. The man's disappointment at losing such a chance prompted him to revenge. He hurried ahead to the royal kraal to lay his complaint and when the tired, almost dying, white men presented themselves to Gungunyana, they were faced with the disappointed swain's accusation of their having raped his girl-friend.

Through Doyle, who could only just speak, the emaciated Doctor pointed to his haggard companions and, shivering with fever, asked, "Do we look like men who desire women?"

Gungunyana had to admit they did not, and the charge was laughed out of court.

The activities at Gungunyana's kraal, when Jameson arrived, were nearly as feverish as the travellers themselves. Captain Pawley and his men had just staggered in with the first load of guns and Mr. Stevens had already handed over the golden sovereigns. The rifles and ammunition were being distributed regardlessly to the ostrich-feathered warriors, and the Portuguese officials waiting on Gungunyana in their gaudy uniforms, complete with epaulettes and spurs—but no horses—were in an understandable state of panic. There was the usual collection of miscellaneous white men hanging round the kraal on the off chance of a concession and, to heighten the tumult, a thunderstorm burst overhead every few hours.

With the delivery of the rifles and the sovereigns, Gungunyana's agreement to grant a concession to the Company was never in doubt, but he probably would not have signed it if Jameson had not been there. Captain Pawley might have wrung it out of him with the help of his troopers—if the Portuguese had let him—but Jameson, even in his rags and his fever, had a far stronger weapon in his personality.

The concession that Gungunyana granted to Jameson was a remarkable document—far more generous than Lobengula's concession to Rudd—and it stands as a monument to the little doctor's strange career of diplomacy with native chiefs. It covered Gazaland and Manicaland—in fact, all Portuguese East Africa between the Zambesi and the Limpopo—and would have been almost without price for the Chartered Company if Gungunyana had ever really owned what it so lavishly gave away. It cost the Company ten thousand pounds and for many years stood as an anachronistic asset on their books. In the end they must have written it off, for Gazaland and most of Manicaland still belong to the Portuguese to-day.

The projected return of the *Countess of Carnarvon* to Chai Chai solved Jameson's problem of what to do with his patients. Moodie had shaken off the worst of the fever, but was certainly no good for a seven hundred mile walk back to Salisbury. Doyle was still very ill. They rigged Doyle up on a stretcher and, dropping down once more into the low veld, they splashed their way through another fifty miles of swamp to the Limpopo.

The *Countess of Carnarvon* riding at anchor in midstream was a refreshing sight. Less comforting was the *Maréchal Macmahon* lying close astern, one gun trained on the wayward *Countess* and the other on the landing stage.

Captain Pawley and his men, with an unusual show of conscience, scuttled into the bush. Jameson called to one of the troopers and, extracting the precious concession from under his rags, handed it over with summary instructions to take it to Port Elizabeth. The man must have been a little surprised to receive a peremptory order, whispered in the shadow of a mopani bush, to run off with a piece of paper and deliver it somewhere five hundred miles away. However, in mitigation, Jameson gave him the two horses —which had miraculously survived the journey and would have been an embarrassment on the ship anyway—and, although the trooper had to travel many miles upstream before he could ford the Limpopo, he was in Port Elizabeth before the doctor.

No Portuguese gunboat could intimidate Jameson and, helped by Moodie, he carried Doyle down to the landing stage and called openly to the *Countess* for a boat to take them off. When Doyle had been lifted painfully on board, they found the ship in the hands of the Portuguese and were all taken prisoner.

The *Maréchal Macmahon*, cruising smoothly up the coast with her now untrammelled bottom, had seen the *Countess* enter the river the second time and, once more, pass the customs without so much as a ladylike nod. It was ungallant to be suspicious of a lady, particularly one flaunting the Blue Ensign, but the *Maréchal* followed her in. When the *Countess* anchored at the landing stage, where some of the cases of rifles were still lying flagrantly in the sun, the gunboat officiously exerted her authority and, despite Captain Buckingham's unctuous protests, put a Portuguese crew on board and struck the Blue Ensign. It was an incident without parallel in the history of the two European powers, and would have delighted the heart of Manuel Antonio de Souza.

When Jameson and his party came aboard, the rest of the crew and passengers of the *Countess* were transferred to the gunboat. Only Doyle and he were allowed to stay—Doyle because he was too ill to be moved again, and Jameson because he put on his Resident-Medical-Officer manner and refused to be separated from his insured interest. His status as a prisoner was a new experience although, in time, he was to make quite a habit of getting himself arrested by foreign states for acts of piracy against them.

By the time the two ships reached Port Elizabeth, the international position was normal again, and it was Jameson who was the hero, and the Portuguese—whose country had been flagrantly violated—who were made to appear the guilty parties.

Jameson's two journeys were his last attempt to bring to fulfilment Johnson's and his own dream of a seaport for Rhodesia. They were abortive attempts because they were never properly planned, and in themselves had no particular fixed objective. Anyone could have told him where the sea was without having to go and find it.

But at least he stirred himself and attempted something practical. For the last sixty years Rhodesians have talked about the crying need for a port, but nobody has set off in a canoe and a singlet to look for one.

X

THERE was one more little act to be played out before the British in Mashonaland and the Portuguese in Mozambique sorted themselves out into the comfortable pattern that still exists to-day. At a high-powered conference in London—where decisions on African affairs were taken more calmly, albeit not so realistically—the Portuguese had agreed to allow peaceful citizens and their goods to travel through the country to Salisbury, on condition that the marauding armies withdrew from Macequece and stayed quietly behind the frontier, and provided that duty was paid on all goods passing through. To the British authorities in London—who would not be called on to pay the duty—the Portuguese seemed to be behaving handsomely.

Rhodes was not so certain that the Portuguese were sincere in their motives. The little matter of gun-running up the Limpopo had left the local people rather touchy. He resolved to test them out. This time he would see to it that the British would be the injured parties and the Portuguese would be taunted into an act of hostility.

He chose Sir John Willoughby, who had been second in command of the pioneer column, to do the taunting. Willoughby's main qualification for the assignment was a particularly irritating manner. When his friends heard Rhodes' plans, they suggested the whole idea was a little unfair on the wretched Sir John, because the Portuguese might be provoked into shooting at him.

Rhodes faced the possibility with his usual indomitable

courage. He assured them he knew the Portuguese and there was nothing to worry about. "They will only shoot him in the leg," he said consolingly.

Rhodes had more respect for the influence of the aristocracy than for the aristocracy itself. Sir John Christopher Willoughby, the fifth baronet, could be a valuable pawn. He was an Eton and Trinity man and an officer in the Blues. If he were shot, even in the leg, there would be a gratifying outcry against the Portuguese in the most influential circles.

Once more, recourse was made to the maritime provisions of the Charter and quite a fleet put out to sea, this time from Durban. One of the Union Company's steamships, the *Norseman*, sailed up the coast with a tug—the *Agnes*, towing three lighters—and a little launch, the *Shark*.

Willoughby was aboard the *Norseman* with three more Englishmen—mere commoners and pawns of little account —and a hundred natives. The lighters carried an innocuous cargo of stores and material for making roads. The natives served to emphasize the law-abiding purpose of the expedition, which was the only reason they were brought along, for they could have had little political value even if the Portuguese did shoot at them.

In fact, Sir John himself was the only target of any value. No one on board was armed, and Willoughby's ostensible orders were to proceed with his gang to the highest navigable point on the Pungwe, and thence to start the inoffensive task of making a road to Salisbury. It was a surprising assignment for a Captain of the Blues.

Nearing Beira, they were intercepted by a Portuguese destroyer which, remembering the indecorous behaviour of the *Countess of Carnarvon*, had reasonable grounds for suspecting the motives of any of the British aristocracy. The destroyer carefully escorted the·expedition into the river, where more of the might of Portugal lay in wait. There were two more destroyers, the *Tamaza* and the *Liberal*, and two gunboats. When Willoughby went ashore at Beira, he was treated with pointed frigidity by the authorities although the people and troops found it more difficult to control their Latin vehemence. He assumed the irritating pose of an Englishman among a lot of half-witted foreigners, and flaunted his ship's manifests before the customs officers, challenging them to inspect the cargoes.

The customs men pretended no desire to see the cargoes. With an unnatural self-control they even refused the tantalizing golden sovereigns Willoughby poured out before them in a fruitless attempt to pay the customs dues. For two long days they resisted his entreaties—and their own natural inclination to take the money—and in the end he gave up.

It was only a few weeks since the insignificant remnants of the army of the Tagus had struggled back to the coast after the battle of Chua Hill and the Portuguese had their own idea of the sincerity of any peaceful pretensions on the part of the British. They adamantly refused to acknowledge that Willoughby had any right to proceed up the river, whether he was taking an army or a road gang.

This was what Rhodes had hoped to happen. This was why he had chosen and sent an English baronet, and provided him with plenty of money, so that there could be no doubt of his readiness to honour the bargain struck in London. Now the Portuguese had put themselves in the wrong by refusing to accept the proffered customs dues. It only remained for them to compound their felony by shooting Willoughby in the leg, and it was up to the unfortunate Sir John to provoke them.

At three o'clock on the third afternoon the *Agnes*, with Sir John conspicuous on the bridge, started to move upstream with two lighters in tow. The little *Shark* preceded her. The might of the Portuguese navy was at battle stations waiting to pounce. The flagship, *Liberal*, ranged herself alongside the *Agnes* and the gunboat *Limpopo* took station on her other beam. Another destroyer, the *Tamaza*, swung across her bows, disturbing the sultry peace of the afternoon with a couple of rounds of blank shot.

From his uncomfortably exposed position on the bridge, Willoughby could see the vessels on each beam of the *Agnes*, not a cable's length away, loading their guns with rounds that looked suspiciously live. He felt that even though they might be aimed only to hit him on the leg, any further attempt to uphold the right of entry into the Pungwe would be injudicious.

The *Agnes* was manned by a scratch crew whose behaviour, on the voyage up the coast, had not been remarkable for its discipline, but when Willoughby now gave orders to stop and proceed astern, they were acted on with commendable alacrity. There seemed no particular object in remaining at Beira, and the fleet, retiring to Durban in creditably good order, was shepherded down the coast by a strong deputation from the Portuguese navy.

The British press in South Africa, taking their cue from Rhodes, clamoured for war to wipe out this insult to British prestige and punish the shocking breach of a solemn agreement between Britain and Portugal. It needed to employ little journalistic originality, for it merely had to say of Portugal what the Lisbon press had been saying of Britain only a few months before.

War with Portugal would offer the one chance of making sure of a sea port for Rhodesia. Unfortunately, the British Navy came along and settled the whole trouble peacefully, as was its wont in the days when the British Navy ruled the seas.

Her Majesty's cruiser *Magicienne* sailed into Beira Bay; the Portuguese gunboats obsequiously dressed ship, and the Governor-General of Mozambique, over copious glasses of the Navy's best gin, declared himself only too happy to allow the passage of peaceful citizens through his country to Mashonaland, and to take their customs dues.   After that, there was no decent excuse left that might justify an attempt to capture Beira.

When Sir John Willoughby returned from his fruitless trip up the coast, he travelled tŏ Pretoria to meet Dr. Jameson.   There was some trouble brewing over yet another concession, and Jameson could be relied on to be in the thick of the argument.

The concession was one which a Dutchman named Adendorff claimed to have obtained from a chief in the Banyai territory, just north of the Limpopo in the southern portion of Matabeleland.   It was low veld country and of little attraction to the pioneer settlers, but the Chartered Company looked on the Limpopo as its southern boundary.

Adendorff said the concession had been given him by the chief, Chibi.   He claimed that the concession gave him prior rights because Chibi was independent of Lobengula —which last assertion was, at the time, strictly true, because Lobengula had had him flayed alive some years before. Some of the terms of the alleged concession were novel. Adendorff and his Boers were said to have promised the chief protection from Lobengula—not a very original undertaking—and in addition to have offered to pay fifty good head of cattle for every beast lost in raids by the Matabele.   If Chibi had been alive, and in good grace with the King, it would certainly have been well worth his while to grant the concession, and then come to some profitable working arrangement with Lobengula.

Dr. Jameson had gone to Pretoria to prove to President Kruger that any such concession must be invalid as Lobengula had already granted all that area along the north bank of the Limpopo in Matabeleland to the Chartered Company.   By some mismanagement, Willoughby went in to see the President first.   Assuming his most irritating manner, he said, "President Kruger, any attempt by the Boers to cross the Limpopo would be tantamount to war,

not only against the Chartered Company, but also against
Her Majesty's Government."

The old President took the threat with commendable
calm. He did say—in Dutch, which Willoughby could
not understand—"If there must be war, let there be war,"
but the interpreter thought it best left unrepeated. As soon
as Willoughby had stalked off from his presence, Kruger
sent a message to the British Agent asking by what
authority a Captain of the Blues threatened the Republic
of the Transvaal.

The British Agent was not too sure—the situation was
not one on which he had instructions—and he had to ask
the High Commissioner in Cape Town.

The High Commissioner, however, had no doubts on
the matter. He cabled, "Disown Willoughby and say Her
Majesty's Government disown him altogether." It was
perhaps a little harsh on a man who had just been put up
by his country to be shot at by the Portuguese.

Then Jameson went to see Kruger and, as always in the
diplomatic field, got his way. Kruger promised to discourage his Boers from fomenting trouble in Matabeleland.
But his discouragement was either half-hearted or ineffec-
tual for, in June 1891, a hundred Boers with thirty or forty
wagons gathered threateningly on the southern bank of the
Limpopo. They were led by Commandant Ignatius Ferreira, who had once fought with the British in the Zulu
war. It was the Boer custom to band together in unofficial
commandos and to follow a chosen leader who assumed
high military rank without any tiresome formalities.

To meet this momentous threat, a force of Bechuanaland
Border Police moved from Macloustie, and the British
South Africa Company's garrison at Tuli rode to join them.
At the main drift across the river, the only point where
the wagons might comfortably cross, they set up a machine-
gun post and entrenched themselves along the river bank.

Jameson—once again the ubiquitous Jameson, who was

always in at the death on any worth-while occasion within the hundreds of thousands of square miles of the sub-continent—was already there.   One afternoon, after he had been inspecting defences along the river—as usual, he held no official rank—he returned to the drift to find Ferreira and four Boers under arrest.   Unarmed, they had come quietly across the river to parley with their opposite num-bers, and the sergeant who had been left in charge had, in the contemporary fashion, arrested them on principle.

Although Jameson was frequently subject to arrest him-self, he preferred to settle differences by talking, because in a battle of words he had all the advantages.   He ordered the men's release and went back across the river with them, swimming his horse.   At the other side the Boers stood grouped on the bank waiting angrily for him.

He stood before them in no wise disconcerted, the water dripping from his boots and leggings, and harangued them. He pointed across the river to the maxim gun on the kopje, its fire commanding the drift, and promised them that no man, if he came armed, would reach the other side alive.   It was not the most diplomatic approach to a commando of a hundred land-hungry Boers but, for some reason, they showed no active resentment.   He invited them to come peacefully, and settle in the new land, and swear allegiance to the Queen, and obey the laws Colquhoun was busily drawing up in Salisbury.   Then he swam his horse back across the river, and Commandant Ferreira went with him and joined the service of the Company.

Adendorff had said, "The God of Heaven, who adminis-ters all things, can alone put a stop to this trek, but man cannot."   In that case it cannot have been Jameson who turned the Boers back, but it was a remarkable coincidence that they gave up the idea next day and turned southward to their homes in the Transvaal.

A couple of months later, the good ship *Norseman* sailed once more up the coast to Beira, this time with the great

Rhodes himself on board, making his first visit to the country that was soon to bear his name. Major Johnson was with him to show him the way up the Pungwe, but Johnson no longer thirsted for the hazards of river transport and the unsinkable boat had been pensioned off, or more probably had descended to its predestined underwater doom.

When they arrived at Beira the Portuguese were determined to show Rhodes how faithfully they were observing both the spirit and letter of the London agreement, and they subjected his personal luggage to an exaggerated examination. Rhodes never carried loose cash with him and they showed unflattering reluctance to accept his personal cheque for the customs dues. He looked on their petty officiousness as symbolic of the way this foreign state blocked the entry to Mashonaland, and he said angrily to Johnson, " I'll take their damned country from them yet." Coming from the Colossus of Africa, it was a singularly impotent threat.

There were other inhabitants of that part of Africa who showed no better respect for the great person of Rhodes. One night, on the journey up the banks of the Pungwe, he felt an urge to leave the tent he shared with Johnson and, with the usual modesty of the great, moved into the bush as far as possible from the light of the camp fire. Johnson had warned him of the awful fate of Beauman, who had been eaten in that very neighbourhood but, somewhat illogically, Rhodes had said, " If I want to see a lion I'll go to the Zoo." Whether he actually saw a lion is not on record, but Johnson heard an unmistakable leonine grunt from the direction Rhodes had gone, and the Prime Minister of the Cape flung himself back into the tent without having stopped to complete the usual seemly adjustments to his dress.

At the border of Mashonaland, Jameson was there to welcome Rhodes into his new country. It was a memorable meeting for these two men who, in the long evenings at Kimberley, had talked so much of the mysterious north. In those days Jameson had shown only a casual interest in the whole fantastic idea. The dreams and plans had all come from Rhodes. Now it was Jameson who had made the dreams reality. It was Jameson who could say to Rhodes, "Come and see what I have done," and it was Jameson who took him along in a rattling old mule cart, over the last ridges of the Marandellas hills and, pointing to the wattle-and-daub huts and wood-and-iron shanties, forlorn in the emptiness of the Mashonaland veld, said, "There's Salisbury."

Rhodes was shockingly disappointed. The worst of being a visionary is that reality often falls so far short of the dream. As they bumped over the pot holes in the only street of the capital city of this new jewel he had set in the Imperial crown, Rhodes looked sadly depressed. Then Jameson pointed out some foundations that were being laid for the Jewish synagogue. Rhodes' depression vanished in a flash, and a great light of confidence shone from his face.

"My country's all right," he cried. "If the Jews come, my country's all right."

Then he met the citizens, who lost no time in telling him what was wrong with it. He was not even allowed time to finish a bath after his journey. As soon as they heard that Rhodes had actually arrived among them, the Vigilance Committee sent the first of many deputations with their grievances, and they found him sitting naked in a tub in the middle of Jameson's hut.

He heard what they had to say while he sponged the grime of the veld from his great body. Not even the un-dignified attitude enforced by a cramped bath could cloud the Rhodes vision. With his knees up to his chin he said, "You must remember that what we are doing here in this country is for the Empire and for posterity."

The Scots leader of the deputation was a realist. "I'll

ha'e ye ken, Mr. Rhodes," he replied, "I'm no' here for posterity."

Dr. Jameson had now been appointed Administrator. Colquhoun had resigned the office even before his year's contract had expired. His civil service outlook had served well enough to draft the laws and ordnances of the new country, but something more human was wanted to enforce them, particularly among men for whom the main attraction of the country had been its potential independence, and freedom from the growing restraints of civilization.

Jameson was a doctor, not a lawyer. He had no experience of administration, and certainly no knowledge of the principles of government. So he started off with every chance of a success. He took on the duties of a cabinet minister and high-court judge rolled into one, and ruled a motley collection of unsettled settlers with little more equipment than an almost proverbial understanding of humanity, and an unassailable sense of humour. In the words of Melina Rorke: "He was thin and insignificant with just a fringe of dark hair below his shining bald dome, but no one ever thought about his looks, so big was his heart, so inspiring his enthusiasm, so great his charm."

He had two main preoccupations—to preserve law and order and to keep down expenses, two almost incompatible aims. The maintenance of law and order had become a sore problem, particularly as the need for economy entailed almost complete disbandment of the police force. Rhodes' critics in Europe were only too ready to expose and exaggerate the lawlessness of his experiment of importing civilization into the wilds of central Africa.

The pioneers themselves had been picked men and decent enough citizens, but many of the adventurers who followed in their tracks—attracted by the prospect of a quick fortune to be made in a wild country—had little time for the niceties of organized society. With men like them, prosperity—even continued existence—soon became dependent on being quick on the draw. In a wide, empty country, where evidence can conveniently be buried out of the likely path of any human, to get away with murder was easy. And it is a sad reflection on the human race that full advantage is usually taken of any such facility.

To Jameson fell the task of calling a halt to this unpleasant tendency. He accomplished his purpose surely enough—by hanging for murder a man who appeared most unlikely to have committed the crime for which he paid the penalty.

A Jew named Andries, carrying a meagre stock of goods with which he intended to open a store in Salisbury, came into the country from the south. He travelled up in a wagon with its owners, two Dutch brothers. There was another man in the party, an Englishman. Of what went on between the members of the party during the long journey, nothing is known, but one morning the Englishman was shot dead, lying in the wagon—which was outspanned—and by uncommon chance his death became known to other travellers before his body had been disposed of in the bush, in the approved style. A motive for the murder was never established, although it was not seriously expected that that could have been important.

The two Dutchmen, with their rifles, had gone that morning into the bush ostensibly to shoot game, and Andries—so he maintained—had taken a walk from the wagon because, not unreasonably, he wanted to be alone. A shot was heard and, by a remarkable coincidence, the Dutchmen and the Jew arrived back at the wagon breathlessly at the same time, although the two brothers had announced their intention of going some way away. They found the Englishman shot through the head, with a revolver near the body. There was a reasonable possibility that Andries had shot him, and there was an equally reasonable possibility that one of the Dutchmen had shot him. It was quite evident he had not shot himself. The police came on the scene and, because it was the first time a murder and a possible suspect had been found together, someone had to be arrested. Not unexpectedly, the choice fell on the little Jew.

A doctor was sent to examine the body but, when he gave evidence at the trial, it transpired he had overlooked the elementary precaution of determining whether the man had been killed by a rifle or revolver bullet. The body had been buried in the veld over a hundred miles from Salisbury and the court thought it unnecessary to go to the trouble of looking for it and examining it again—particularly as it would probably never be found.

Having no reliable evidence as to which weapon had done the deed, the court unhesitatingly accepted that it could not have been one of the Dutchmen's rifles. That Andries had no apparent motive for murdering the Englishman was regarded as irrevelant. There was, too, a significant discrepancy between the evidence of the two brothers. One said they had been away in the bush for half an hour, and the other said it had only been ten minutes. All of which might have planted a seed of doubt in a court used to the weighing of evidence.

It was Jameson's first murder trial. He sat as the Chief Magistrate, with four assessors. When they unanimously found Andries guilty—on evidence so slender and questionable that no properly constituted British court of justice could possibly have upheld the charge—let alone the conviction—it is possible they were thinking more of the imperative need for law and order, and they weighed the wretched little man's life against the innumerable lives that would inevitably be sacrificed if the current lawlessness continued.

It was not justice, but it was courageous. When Jameson pronounced sentence of death by hanging, it was not the prisoner who collapsed, but the magistrate, and he had to be carried from the court.

Andries was executed in public in Salisbury's Cecil Square where the jacarandas blossom so brightly to-day, and at night coloured lights play on the fountain. It was a crude performance without any of the humane refinements of a modern execution. It was the only time a white man was hanged in Rhodesia for sixty years, the privilege having been meanwhile reserved exclusively for the natives. If Andries' execution was nothing more than a sacrificial rite, it served its purpose, for from then on the white men in Mashonaland appeared to be effectively discouraged from actually killing each other.

XI

THE final conquest of Lobengula's country, known as the Matabele War, can hardly lay claim to the status of a full-scale campaign, as the name suggests. Of the contending armies one was less than seven hundred strong, and the war was fought and won in two skirmishes, each lasting little more than an hour. In these one-sided battles the Matabele, whose numbers might well have been overwhelming, were decimated and the white men suffered but half a dozen casualties. The disaster of the Shangani Patrol followed after the war had virtually been won, and is a story of its own.

For nearly three years after the pioneers came to Mashonaland, Lobengula kept himself unobtrusively in the background. He used to send out his raiding parties among the Mashonas in case they were tempted to adopt any false notions that he was no longer their master—a boon he was determined they were to continue to enjoy so that he could go on exacting tribute from them in cattle and women.

For the most part these raids were unnoticed by the white men as Mashonaland was still a wide and empty country, and the new settlers actually saw little of the legendary Matabele. Jameson's policy was to keep on the right side of his old friend Lobengula, for he was one of the few white men in the country who had seen with his own eyes the massed might of the King's impis. He made Lobengula a present of an unpromising gold reef in the Hartley district, and equipped the mine with a steam engine whose lack of tractive power was offset by the bright green paint on the boiler, with the King's name picked out in gilt capitals on either side. That the mine was unlikely to prosper was unimportant. Lobengula had no use for gold anyway, but the gesture gave Jameson a comfortable feeling—which was entirely unwarranted—that Lobengula had been flattered into forgetting his annoyance at the white men's intrusion in his country.

Rhodes, too, was quite convinced that things had been settled amicably with the King. As late as November in 1892, two years after the occupation, he declared in a speech, "We are on the most friendly terms with Lobengula. He receives a globular sum of a hundred pounds a month in sovereigns, and he looks forward with great satisfaction to the day of the month when he will receive them. I have not the least fear of any trouble in the future from Lobengula."

Perhaps this was hopeful thinking on Rhodes' part, born of his conviction that every man has his price—although the globular sum might have seemed a small price for a Matabele king—and his certainty that the Company could never afford a war.

Twelve months before Rhodes made this sanguine announcement, a prominent Mashona chief, Lomagundi, had been killed by the Matabele because he had refused to pay tribute to Lobengula and, worst crime of all, had suggested that now the white men were in the country Lobengula no longer held sway. Jameson was compelled to protest against the murder because Lomagundi and his people were working with the settlers, and there was a certain aversion among the white men to witnessing the native practice of disembowelment. Jameson sent Lobengula a message in the style of the occupying powers in Berlin, just after the last world war, protesting to Russia over a frontier infringement, and Lobengula's answer was correspondingly evasive and unsatisfactory.

There was another incident in 1892, when a Mashona chief playfully cut away five hundred yards of Rhodes' precious telegraph wire. For this offence he was summarily ordered by Jameson to pay a fine in cattle. Because there was better pasturage in Mashonaland, Lobengula was in the habit of sending cattle to be grazed by Mashona tribes—as part of their tribute—and the chief thriftily used some of these to pay the fine.

Lobengula discovered the fraud, and naturally the embezzler accused the white men of seizing the royal cattle against his will. Lobengula sent a protest to the High Commissioner in Cape Town and the affair had all the makings of a first class international incident.

When explanations were over and the true offender was revealed, Lobengula meted out punishment in his traditional style and the chief and many of his tribe met a grisly fate. Once more Jameson protested at the entry of armed Matabele into his country, but Lobengula, his authority strengthened by the incident, blandly replied that while the white men in Mashonaland might suffer under the laws of the Company, all the natives—in Mashonaland as well as Matabeleland—still enjoyed his own rule, and that nothing that had taken place in the long negotiations between them had ever gainsaid that. It was a nice constitutional point, and happened to be quite right.

In July of 1893, Lobengula sent a modest force of two thousand five hundred warriors to impose the process of his law on a recalcitrant chief whose kraal was but a few miles from the rapidly growing white settlement of Fort Victoria. The commander of his force interpreted his orders liberally and, within forty-eight hours of his arrival in the district, all the Mashonas and Makalangas who were working for the white men had either fled in terror or had been ardently butchered. For the settlers, such a thorough massacre on their doorsteps was both inconvenient and unpleasant and, although the Matabele pointedly left the

white people untouched, they hinted that their turn was
to come, which was unnerving.

In all fairness to Jameson and Rhodes, neither had
wanted trouble with the Matabele. Some of the more
ambitious prospectors had found their way across the border,
attracted, as ever, by land out of sight over the hill. To a
man looking for gold—or anything else for that matter—the
brightest prospects are always just ahead. Jameson summarily forbade them to cross the border and thereby planted
yet another grievance against the autocracy of the Company. When the Matabele failed to reciprocate, Jameson's
policy of appeasement was more unpopular than ever.

But Jameson was never a man to fear consequences and
when he heard of the ugly developments at Fort Victoria
he knew the time had come to talk to Lobengula in his
own language. He hurried south to the town, to find all
the white population huddled in the doubtful security of
the fort. As the Administrator he at last had an official
position, even if it were not a military one. Without hesitation he took command, and ordered Lendy, the military
officer in charge of the district, to arrange a meeting with
the commander of the Matabele impi.

At noon the next day, sitting in a kitchen chair in front
of the fort, with Lendy at his side and a bodyguard of
armed settlers grouped behind him, Jameson received the
old warrior, Manyao. Jameson had sat too long under the
indaba tree at Bulawayo not to know the proper etiquette.
There were long formal salutations and, when these were
over, he assured Manyao, in his most obliging tone, that he
was quite capable of governing his country without the
assistance of the Matabele.

Manyao, with the innate courtesy of his Zulu forefathers,
pointed out how wrong Jameson was. Surprisingly, he
seemed to know all about the Rudd Concession, and he
reminded Jameson that in that curious document Lobengula had been named King of Mashonaland and that the

only powers given to the white men had been to dig holes in the ground. Leaders of unlettered people often express themselves well, for words are their only traffic in ideas. With simple but effective eloquence Manyao told how, since the days of M'Zilikazi—the father of their people—the Matabele had collected tribute from the Mashonas and the law had decreed that defaulters were punishable by death. It was a law entrenched by precedent. If Manyao's advocacy had been left unassisted, Jameson would have found the Matabele case difficult to answer.

But there is nearly always a hothead to spoil a good cause. When Manyao had finished speaking, an arrogant young chief, Umgandaan, stepped forward and gratuitously informed Jameson that his King had sent him to perform certain duties and no white man would stop him.

Manyao's reasoned statement had disturbed the tough burghers of Fort Victoria, despite themselves, and an uncomfortable quiet had followed his speech, but Umgandaan's truculence restored their enmity for the Matabele like a refreshing gust of wind. Jameson cut him short and ordered Manyao to remove his army across the Tokwe River before sundown, failing which his own soldiers would drive the Matabele out. It was a bold ultimatum of war against a nation that could raise twenty thousand fighting men and Jameson's own fifty soldiers heard it with mixed feelings.

Late that afternoon, the Matabele army that lay at the gates of Fort Victoria had shown no signs of moving. Captain Lendy led out forty of his mounted men—something had to be kept in reserve—and, although the foray turned out to be nothing more than a skirmish, it was probably the most courageous action of the war, for there was no precedent to show how the Matabele hordes would react to rifle fire. There was the unpleasant possibility they would accept a few casualties and then turn and wipe out their attackers by sheer weight of numbers.

In the event, Lendy's men found the Matabele scattered and their attack came as a complete surprise for, in the Matabele theory of war, numbers was the only factor that counted and Lobengula and his people never believed that the few whites in the country would be mad enough to risk a clash. The Matabele were driven across the river and fifty of their number lay dead on the veld—including Umgandaan who, like many hotheads, at least had the courage to die for his beliefs.

Matabeleland had loomed on the Company's horizon for some time as a tantalizing prize, particularly after the legendary gold in Mashonaland had turned out to be so disappointing. Rhodes had coveted the country so much, in fact, that he had taken expert advice on the size of an army that would be needed to conquer it. When he had been told by the best military brains in South Africa that at least seven thousand men would be wanted—an army beyond even his ample means—he had perforce adopted and preached the doctrine of Matabeleland for the Matabele.

But there were some Boers among the settlers at Fort Victoria and they had none of these exaggerated ideas about the size of an army needed to overcome a mob of kaffirs. They remembered how a few mounted men had broken the might of the Zulus. They told Jameson that a thousand men, properly mounted, could rout the Matabele. Jameson caught their enthusiasm and telegraphed Rhodes for his support. A campaign, even with only a thousand men, needed money.

Rhodes, already sensing the call for economy, could hardly have sent a curter reply. " Read Luke xiv. 31," he wired. It was a convenient code, unlikely to be broken by the godless Matabele, and Jameson—when he had found a Bible—read, " Or what king, going to make war against another king, sitteth not down first, and consulteth whether he be able with ten thousand to meet him that cometh against him with twenty thousand?" Jameson, the amateur general, was unimpressed. He carried on his preparations for war and Rhodes perforce had to support him.

Two troops of horsemen were raised, the "Victoria Horse" and the "Salisbury Horse". From the outset, the "Salisbury Horse" could have boasted two hundred and fifty horsemen if it had not been short of two hundred and fifty horses. Badgered by Jameson, who was convinced a swift blow was necessary before the Matabele took the initiative, Rhodes found himself forced to sell fifty thousand of his precious Chartered shares, and his lieutenants spread out over South Africa with orders to buy a thousand horses.

It was an expensive business. Many horses died of horse sickness on the way north. It took three months to equip the invasion force—after the alarm at Fort Victoria, three months of constant anxiety. In the end, the two troops were only able to raise seven hundred mounted men between them. The men's conditions of service were based on the promise of loot—no pay as such, but when the war had been won, six thousand acres of Matabeleland for each man, twenty mining claims, and a share of Lobengula's cattle. Inevitably, when the terms were heard in England, there was a suspicion that Matabeleland was being invaded for the spoils of war.

However, there was some unexpected support from the Imperial authorities in the south. The High Commissioner moved the Bechuanaland Police to the Matabeleland border. History is content to suggest this was a friendly gesture of support for Jameson's army. At the time, neither Rhodes nor Jameson looked on the imperial move in such a happy light. There was the very present danger that Britain would sooner see Matabeleland an extension of the Bechuanaland Protectorate than a new asset for the Chartered Company's shareholders.

The High Commissioner almost confirmed this when he

told Rhodes that naturally any final settlement with Lobengula must be conducted through him. Rhodes replied
tartly that he was paying for the war—which may have been
arrogant, but was at least unanswerable. So, in the age-
old manner of power politics, an imaginary frontier incident was engineered on the banks of the Shashi River, and
the Bechuanaland Border Police moved into Matabeleland. After that, the campaign became a race between
Jameson's army and the Imperial troops to get to Bulawayo
first.

Early in October 1893, almost exactly three years after
the pioneer column had disbanded at Salisbury, the two
troops from Victoria and Salisbury set out and converged at
Iron Mine Hill, near Umvuma, well inside the borders of
Matabeleland. Thence, they moved forward in parallel
lines, and at night laagered with their wagons in the form
of a fort, like the pioneer column of 1890.

But this time they were not to go scatheless and without
a fight. First blood came to the Matabele, before the Victoria column had been joined by the Salisbury force. Captain Campbell, the ordnance officer, was badly wounded and,
for a few hours, Jameson put aside the mantle of amateur
generalship and became once more the professional surgeon. He tried to save Campbell's life by amputating his
leg, but the Captain died the next day. Another casualty
within a few days was Ted Burnett, who had been one of
the transport officers with the pioneer column.

In the Somabula Forest, the Matabele intended to stage
one of their devastating ambushes. They had, in fact, lain
there in great force the night before the columns passed
through. But in the morning there arose a fog—an unusual
phenomenon in that country—and as this could only be
some of the white men's witchcraft, the Matabele fled
in terror across the Shangani River before their enemy
even came in sight. If there had been no fog that morning and the ambush had caught the tiny columns in the

thick bush, the entire male population of white Rhodesia would have been virtually wiped out.

On the south bank of the Shangani, in more open country, Jameson's army found itself surrounded by five thousand Matabele. But here there was room to manœuvre, and with a Hotchkiss gun and a number of Maxims, the Matabele were driven off, leaving at least five hundred dead behind them. Jameson had already started to disprove St. Luke.

It was in this battle that it became more evident what a disservice to the Matabele Rhodes had done when he made them his present of a thousand rifles—although it must be acknowledged that the gift was made with very different motives. Naturally there was a great temptation to challenge the white man with his own devastating weapons, but as the Matabele had never had any training in the use of firearms, the devastation was as extravagant among themselves as among the enemy. They were handicapped, too, by the illusion that the higher the sights were raised the greater the speed and power of the bullets, and as, naturally, they wanted to strike as hard as they could, the theory tended to prejudice their marksmanship. Another unfortunate misconception was that the shells from the Hotchkiss gun carried white men into their midst, who were released among them when the shells exploded, and a lot of ammunition and effort were expended in firing at the bursts.

If the Matabele had only followed their traditional methods of war that had served their Zulu forefathers so well, they might well have overrun Jameson's army at one charge. As it was, the warriors who were put out in front as the spearhead of the attack, instead of rushing on the enemy with assegai and shield and Zulu ferocity, fumbled with bolts and magazines that were quite beyond their understanding, and became sitting targets for the deadly marksmanship of trained riflemen. They showed no lack

of that reckless courage on which their reputation as a
fighting race had been built. Put to its more wonted
use, in massed charges against a handful of lightly
armed men, their irresistible onslaught might well have
annihilated the white men, leaving the unprotected
women and children in the towns to an even more grisly
fate.

For there was no second line of defence, and there were
no reserves. It was a situation which would have shocked
Churchill as he was shocked in 1940, when the Germans
were breaking through, and he asked General Gamelin,
"But where is the strategic reserve?" and Gamelin
answered, "It does not exist." In 1893, in Matabeleland,
every able-bodied white man was with the two vulnerable
little columns, hurrying to Bulawayo before the Imperial
troops marched in and put the riches of Lobengula's country
out of their reach. Like Gamelin, Jameson did not believe
in strategic reserves.

Fortunately, none were required. The second battle,
if such the slaughter can be called, was fought at Bembesi,
north of Thabas Induna, the little flat hill that rises within sight of Bulawayo. What Lobengula had feared for
years was happening and the English chameleon was flick-
ing out its long devouring tongue. He sent out his own
bodyguard of seven hundred invincible warriors and, in
less than an hour, five hundred of these were killed. Sir
John Willoughby witnessed the fight. He said, "The
Umbezu and Ingubu regiments were practically annihilated. I cannot speak too highly of the pluck of these regiments. I believe that no civilized troops could have with-
stood the terrific fire they did for half as long."

On the fourth of November, 1893, a Pipe Major of the
Royal Scots led the column into what was left of the burning city of Bulawayo. To welcome them were two white
traders, Fairbairn and Usher, whom Lobengula, great
gentleman as he was even in defeat, had left in the care of

one of his indunas with strict orders that they should come
to no harm.

Eleven days later, the Imperial column from the south
marched in. But although the Union Jack was already
flying over Lobengula's kraal, it was the Chartered Company, in the person of Dr. Jameson, that ruled from under
the indaba tree. Rhodes had not wasted the cost of his
war.

Britain usually suffers her disasters at the beginning of
her wars and the disasters jerk her out of her apathy and
shame her into winning the last battle. The Matabele War
was a notable exception, for the enemy was decisively
defeated in the first two battles and the conquerors rode
into his capital having lost but half a dozen men. Then, as
the enemy withdrew into the bush, to nurse his grievances
and wait his chance for a guerilla strike three years later,
he inflicted a parting shot on the victors and the war ended
with a disaster that would have been more appropriate to
a traditional beginning.

By our more expansive standards to-day, when battles
embrace much greater numbers, the loss of thirty-three men
would rank merely as an unfortunate incident. But, quite
apart from the major loss it represented in terms of this
miniature campaign, the annihilation of Major Allan Wilson's little force—that came to be known as the Shangani
Patrol—held a terrible significance.

Less than seven hundred men had set forth to do battle
with tens of thousands of savages. Military opinion had
estimated that ten times the number, with up-to-date arms
and equipment, were needed for success. Rhodes, of
course, held this opinion suspect, its only object reputation
and promotion. He said he had no intention of spending
a hundred thousand pounds to make somebody a major-
general. Jameson would do the job for nothing.

Even so, it was due far more to good fortune than to
sound judgment that the seven hundred men met the

enemy's thousands on favourable ground. The subsequent disaster to the Shangani Patrol was but a delayed object lesson of what might have happened to the entire little army if Providence had not guided it to meet the Matabele on open ground.

Even more illuminating, in the light of wisdom after the event, is the revelation of the slender thread of amateur command which held sufficiently to bring a force of untrained volunteers through to Bulawayo because it was never strained. When put to the test, it snapped, and thirty-three brave lives were thrown away. Some say that if Jameson had been with the Shangani Patrol, his resolute will would never have allowed a situation to develop whereby a small force was left unsupported at the mercy of the Matabele hordes. But responsibility must surely rest at the top, and that the disaster came to pass stands as witness to the peril in which every man in the campaign had stood.

When Bulawayo had been occupied, Lobengula and his retreating impis still existed as a menace to peace. A patrol was sent out in pursuit. The patrol would have been strong enough for the job had it been properly equipped and provisioned. But the three hundred volunteers—half from the Mashonaland column and half from the column from the south—were given only three days' rations. They had no wagons to form a laager and, at night, they slept in a hollow square, the men themselves acting as protection for their horses. They were soaked to the skin by the torrential rains that burst upon them. At Inyati, they met a Matabele impi which they drove off, but Major Forbes, who was in command, left behind there eighty men as a garrison—somewhat in contrast with the puny garrisons Forbes had scattered over Portuguese East Africa in the carefree days of 1890. The weakened patrol pushed on into the bush, but their supplies of food were already running short and, not surprisingly, murmurs of discontent started to be heard.

It was a volunteer force—the men were citizens fighting to protect themselves, not levies sent to war by their rulers —and the inducement of loot no longer held, for Matabeleland was already conquered. With lack of inspiration in their commanders, they baulked at sacrificing their lives for a purpose they could no longer recognize as necessary. Lobengula had been defeated, Bulawayo had been taken, and there seemed little obvious need to follow the King into the treacherous bush. Resistance movements had not yet found their way into the military vocabulary, and it was not until three years later that the white people learned the folly of letting the Matabele live to fight another day. Even so, the fault of irresolution was not with them, but with their leaders, who had sent them out ill-equipped to do what was required of them.

When the direct question was put to them by their commander whether they were willing to go on, only about half of them assented, and Major Forbes perforce turned back to Bulawayo. At Shiloh they were met by reinforcements sent out hurriedly by Jameson. The disaffected men were left behind and the re-formed Shangani Patrol, now better provisioned and equipped with wagons and Maxim guns, turned and set out again three hundred strong in pursuit of the King. But the heavy rains persisted, the wagons were but a hindrance to progress, and in the end these had to be left behind with the unmounted men.

When the patrol ultimately reached the Shangani River —now close on the heels of the Matabele—it was but one hundred and sixty strong, and it faced the desperate remains of Lobengula's army with divided councils at its head.

Captain Raaff, who had recruited the Bechuanaland Border Police who formed the column from the south, was a sick man. He was to die of peritonitis but a month later and the disease which hastened his end was already preying on him. Forbes listened to him and shared the doubts his condition engendered, and it was mainly Raaff's forebodings of danger which prompted the fateful decision that left Wilson and his men to their tragic fate.

When they arrived at the Shangani, Forbes sent Major Allan Wilson—who had commanded the Victoria column —across the river with twelve volunteers to keep in touch with the retreating King, with orders to return to the main body before sunset. There was reason to believe that Lobengula was now guarded by an army of at least three thousand warriors.

Wilson made contact with what he thought to be the royal party and, disregarding his orders to return, sent Captain Napier back to the column reporting that he was but half a mile from the King. It was now dark, and Wilson was waiting for daylight. His failure to return as ordered was no dereliction of duty. Nor was the predicament he and his men found themselves in later due to any rashness on his part. He had accomplished what he had been sent out to essay—to find the King and his camp—and he would have been lacking in soldierly initiative if he had abandoned his quarry merely to obey the letter of his orders. He sent a messenger to report the position, and the decision for the next move lay with his commander.

It was then that Forbes made the decision that reflected the weakness in command which had been so happily untested before. He was burdened with Raaff's forebodings that the whole column would be surrounded by the Matabele at any moment, and he feared to cross the Rubicon of the Shangani and commit his whole force to battle. Having recognized the danger of such a step, his clear alternative was to send Napier with a message recalling Wilson and his handful of men. Instead, he sent Captain Borrow and another twenty troopers to follow Wilson, and so committed thirty-six men to a task he had already decided was unsafe for a hundred and sixty.

When Barrow joined Wilson they waited for the dawn— to find themselves surrounded. Knowing their retreat cut off they chose the desperate course of a direct attack at the enemy's strongest point—where the King had lain the night before. But Lobengula had already moved on and in their first brush with his guards they were driven back. Some of them were wounded; some of their horses were killed. They marched back for about a mile, watched from all directions by the Matabele who surrounded them. Their only chance of survival was to fight their way through the encircling enemy.

But that would have meant leaving the wounded behind, so they discarded that, their only hope. Three, chosen for their experience as scouts, were sent to rush the Matabele lines and make a dash for the column to seek reinforcements. These three men, well equipped in courage and knowledge of the bush, broke through to the Shangani now coming down in flood. They themselves were able to swim their horses across the river, but after the storms the water was rising every minute and it was soon out of the question for the rest of the column to cross.

The dash through the lines aroused the Matabele, who now closed in on the thirty-three. Wilson and his men had discussed their position calmly and agreed to stay with the wounded, and they knew now that they could only stand together and die. In a few minutes all the horses—easy targets for assegais—had been killed and they used the bodies for cover. The battle, which started in the early morning, went on all day. Every hour, for twelve hours, two more of them died. As the sun went down half a dozen men were still alive and fighting back. A Matabele who was there told later how these survivors shook each other's hands and then awaited the final attack. When one man only was left, he collected all the ammunition he could find on his fallen comrades and ran to the top of a great ant heap, where he shot it out with his attackers to the inevitable end.

Jameson's laconic telegram to Rhodes tells the story as

it should be told, in stark simplicity. "They fought," he said, "all day, killing a great number of the Matabele; but finished their ammunition, then the Matabele fired at them from close quarters, killing, as they thought, those still alive. After a time they approached nearer and found there were still some alive, all seriously wounded, writing on pieces of paper. As soon as the Matabele came close to them, they drew their revolvers; but the whole thing was very soon finished, and not one of the whole party was left alive."

The remains of the valiant little company were first buried where they fell by the man who ultimately found them and, in the greatness of simplicity, wrote their epitaph on a tree, "To Brave Men." This unaffected tribute is perpetuated on their memorial that stands to-day in the peace of the Matopo Hills, close to the resting place of Rhodes and Jameson.

Meanwhile, Matabeleland had been conquered by the white men and become part of Rhodesia, and Lobengula, the last of the Zulu kings, hid in the veld like one of the subject chiefs he so despised. The great mountain of a man grew thin and weak, and soon he died. The chameleon had devoured the fly.

XII

ALTHOUGH, up to the outbreak of the Boer War, Dr. Jameson had never attested as a soldier, he had already led a military expedition to occupy a country, had taken operational command in a full-scale war, and had conducted an armed invasion into a foreign state, which was a fairly martial record for a civilian. The armed invasion, which was nothing less than an act of unprovoked aggression on a friendly foreign state, was the precursor to arrest on a charge not far short of treason, a sentence of imprisonment, a premiership, a baronetcy, a privy-councillorship, and the immortality of a grave alongside Rhodes in the Matopos.

The invasion has gone down in history as the Jameson Raid, and the only people who know the true facts about it are conveniently dead. It was but an interlude in the history of Rhodesia, although it was a lively episode in the essential story. It was more like a rough and tumble scene that took place in the wings, drawing away for an interval the principal actors in the main play. The audience in Rhodesia could only hear a lot of shouting, a smothered explosion and loud whisperings, intended to explain and mystify at the same time, until the stars were ready to come back on the stage, a little dishevelled certainly, but still endowed with the magic of their art.

There are two subjects of ceaseless dispute in Africa. The two are woven together but they started from separate origins. One started because a civilized race came to settle in a land occupied by savages—the fact that the races had different coloured skins was incidental. The same dispute between civilized European and African savage would have raged even if the Africans had been flaxen-haired blonds. All cats are grey at night, as many a prurient white man has conceded; what made the African native unacceptable to him in broad daylight was his unfortunate behaviour.

The second dispute is far less subtle and has grown up between the white men themselves. The Dutch came to the Cape three hundred years ago and stayed there virtually unmolested for a hundred and fifty years. During that time they established quite a civilization of their own. Then the English came in the early nineteenth century and tried to drive them out, and for the last hundred and fifty years the two have been disputing whose country South Africa really is, and which of their languages they should talk. The Jameson Raid was a resounding shout in the dispute. It might have led to immediate blows, but at the time it did little more than embitter the eternal argument. Nevertheless, the blows followed soon enough when the Boer War broke out a few years later.

When the Dutch had crossed the Vaal about fifty years before, they had set up the Transvaal Republic and in time Paul Kruger became its President. Sir Theophilus Shepstone, in the name of England, had once annexed the republic, but the Boers challenged the might of Britain at Majuba and the whipped lion meekly withdrew. Kruger's people had trekked hundreds of miles into the interior of the continent to get away from kaffirs and Englishmen only, in the end, to find themselves pursued by the Scots. For the richest goldfield in the world poked its vulgar outcrop through the homely veld of their new land, and Scotsmen, Jews and Gentiles of nearly every nationality, came in their thousands. Rhodes and his English friends came tumbling over each other too—although a little belatedly in the scramble for claims. Between 1885 and 1895, eighty thousand adult males from various parts of the world came to the Transvaal, outnumbering the humble burghers by four to one. In Kruger's eyes they were all foreigners, which was not an unreasonable view for the head of a sovereign state to take.

Nevertheless, the foreigners tended to resent his refusal to allow them any rights of citizenship because, between them, they were paying most of the taxes. Their liability —as also their ability—to pay the taxes arose, of course, from the happy presence of a source of wealth that belonged to the country which had the temerity to tax them. But there was little said of that outside Pretoria, where Kruger ruled in puritanical aloofness. From the noisy saloons of Johannesburg—and particularly from the bar of the Rand Club—the cry went out for " the preservation of those public liberties without which life is not worth having ". Those were the actual words of a letter that was to appeal to Jameson—who, by a remarkable coincidence, was waiting on the frontier of the Republic with quite a little army—to come to the rescue of " thousands of men, women and children of our race who will be at the mercy of well-armed Boers ". The letter added, rather more feelingly, that " property of enormous value will be in the greatest peril ".

This menace of a few fatherly Boers was an alarming prospect for those thousands of foreigners whose main complaint was that they were the biggest majority anyway, and who had been sedulously importing rifles and ammunition disguised as mining supplies. For a long time someone had been indulging in an enterprising piece of smuggling in oil drums with false bottoms. Sufficient oil was put in the bottom to start flowing out from the drum if some officious person turned the drain-cock. In the manner of Chesterton's rolling English road, the drums went from Kimberley to Johannesburg by way of Port Elizabeth, for it would have been difficult to explain away repeated shipments of oil from Mr. Rhodes' diamond mine in Kimberley direct to his gold mine in Johannesburg.

The letter calling Jameson to the aid of the oppressed foreigners in Johannesburg he actually drafted himself during an unobtrusive visit to the town. He seems to have found his friends in the city not unduly weighed down by their thraldom and without any particular impatience to be rescued from it. But he persuaded them to sign the letter and, more important, to leave it undated. With an unusual concern for the financial interests of the Company, he made them insert in the letter, "We guarantee any expense that may be incurred by you in helping us."

He carried it off in his pocket and, so that there could be no misunderstanding, he went all the way to Cape Town—a thousand miles there and a thousand miles back—to show it exultantly to Rhodes.

Then he returned to the little army he, the civilian Administrator of Rhodesia, had collected so painstakingly in the middle of Bechuanaland, on the border of the Transvaal, at its nearest point to Johannesburg.

Here, at the little post office station known as Pitsani Botluko, Jameson waited all too impatiently for the events to happen that would justify the burning words of the letter which said, "the circumstances are so extreme that we cannot but believe that you and the men under you will not fail to come to the rescue". It was an appeal no true soldier —even though he were not attested—could resist, and when the time for action did at last come, he took the letter, carefully filled in an arbitrary date, and sent it forth on a journey that ended up in the august columns of the London *Times*. The events it deplored, of course, never happened.

If the letter's poignant appeal had to be answered, Jameson's little army in Bechuanaland could hardly have been more fortuitously placed. The railway line from Mafeking to Bulawayo, carefully skirting the western border of the Transvaal, was being laid at the time, and, although many hundreds of miles of railway had already been built in Southern Africa with little apparent danger to the people engaged, the perils inherent in this particular stretch of line were so great that there were needed to protect it five hundred trained soldiers, eight maxims and three field guns. At least, that was the army Dr. Jameson, the chief magistrate of Rhodesia, had collected in the closing months of 1895, nearly five hundred miles outside the borders of his sphere of authority. There had been some tentative arrangements with the Colonial Office for the Company to take over a strip of Bechuanaland, but these were unconvincing, and hardly supplied a valid excuse for armed incursion. Perhaps it was but a realization of the true extent of the danger that prompted this force not to spread out along the line it was guarding but kept itself bunched together in the little village of Pitsani for over two months and then, when it moved, to strike out right away from the railway.

By a fortuitous chain of circumstances, the Company which, up to but a few months before, had been economizing rigorously, had now sanctioned an increase in the police establishment owing to certain undefined responsibilities incurred in Barotseland. But, instead of being sent north of the Zambesi, where Barotseland lay, these new policemen found themselves, somehow, five hundred miles to the south, in Bechuanaland; and Barotseland, as a happy outcome, was left eventually to be occupied by a force of twelve unarmed civilians.

However, the new establishment gave Jameson, as his second in command, Sir John Willoughby, he of the Blues and the irritating manner. There were, too, other officers from crack British regiments—from the Welch Fusiliers, the Scots Fusiliers, the Life Guards, the Grenadier Guards, the Royal Artillery, the Seaforth Highlanders and the 6th Dragoons—to name but a few. The War Office seemed to raise little objection to its front line officers burying themselves in the heart of Africa to guard a railway line.

Unfortunately, the revolutionary ardour of the oppressed people in Johannesburg hardly matched the eagerness for action of their would-be saviours. Somehow there seemed to be lacking among them any passionate faith in their cause. Perhaps it was the cause that was luke-warm and not the revolutionaries. Even among themselves, many of those who were palpably agitating against Kruger and all he stood for, held that revolt—if it came—should come under his own flag, the Vierkleur. To have raised the Union Jack in the heart of the Transvaal would have been a little foolhardy, for even republics are jealous of their sovereignty and look askance on treason. Jameson was waving it vigorously enough on the border, but none in Johannesburg waved in reply, and when they sent two urgent messengers to his camp at Pitsani—they sent them by different routes to make sure the message arrived—it was not to urge him to hurry to their succour, but to tell him for heaven's sake not to come.

But Jameson was not one to be discouraged by people reluctant to be saved. The two emissaries, Captains Holden and Heany, had not been screened as a security risk, as we say to-day, too carefully. Both were officers of the Rhodesian police. Heany had gone with the pioneer column to Salisbury in 1890 and had served with Jameson through the Matabele War, so his partialities should not have been much in doubt. Holden, in Kimberley, had been mainly responsible for the little matter of oil drums with false bottoms.

Heany was sent with the urgent message from Johannesburg by special train and, arriving at Mafeking, twenty-five miles from Pitsani, at half-past four on a Sunday morning, he woke up an unfortunate storekeeper, bought a pair of field-boots and a kitbag, and somehow acquired a horse. None of these were absolute necessities for the short journey to Pitsani, as there was plenty of transport offering. Afterwards he explained them away, a little unconvincingly, by saying he might have found Jameson already gone and would have had to follow him across-country.

Holden had been sent from Johannesburg on horseback, and—the railways of those days being no better than they are to-day—had justified the precaution by arriving before Heany's train. It was a ride of a hundred and seventy miles and it took him three days. The two officers found Jameson still at Pitsani, impatient for action, and they faithfully discharged the mission entrusted to them by delivering their message calling on him not to enter the Transvaal. Then, their duty done, they went in with him.

History has encouraged the fiction that nobody but Dr. Jameson himself ever wanted to use his little army for an invasion into the Transvaal, and that the fiasco of the Raid was but the bitter fruit of his own impulsiveness. Everybody else concerned, particularly in the high places in Britain, is said to have moved heaven and earth to stop him or to have known nothing of his intentions until it was too late. In all the best chronicles of these events no mention is made of the spate of cables that had been passing for months between London, Johannesburg and Cape Town. In the three capitals, the fiction that was to be perpetuated was carefully built up. Even at the top, the Colonial Secretary in Britain, and the High Commissioner in South Africa, who were both well aware of what was afoot, strove manfully to maintain official ignorance.

The Colonial Secretary was Joseph Chamberlain, in the first stages of his metamorphosis from municipal radical to imperialist jingo. He had risen to the councils of the Empire on the ladder of Birmingham gas, water and sewerage. They called him "Radical Joe" because, in his struggle up the ladder, he had denounced government by privilege. Now, he was already on the way to becoming the champion of privileged imperialism.

The Secretary of the Chartered Company was one Dr. Rutherfoord Harris who, like Jameson, had been in practice in Kimberley. But he had shown more interest in shooting, and gambling in gold shares, than in medicine, to the detriment of his pocket, and somehow he had found his way into the service of the Company in Salisbury. He was not particularly popular with the settlers, mainly because of the current suspicion that he had been found an easy job. One day, when he was indulging his craze for shooting, he was mauled by a crocodile, and he had to be sent hurriedly south for proper treatment. His assailant might fittingly have joined in the tears that were shed at his departure.

He found himself more in his own element among those manipulating the fortunes of the Company at the top and, appointed Secretary, he was equally involved in its affairs in Cape Town and London. In August, only four months before the Raid, he had sought out Chamberlain in London for an interview and, in the presence of a formidable gathering of political eminence, had drawn his attention to the unrest in Johannesburg. It is on record that he added " a guarded allusion to the desirability of there being a police force near the border ". When Chamberlain showed no adverse reaction to this startling proposal, he took a chance and went on conspiratorially, " I could tell you something in confidence."

This was presuming too much on official tractability and Chamberlain, who had heard all he wanted to know, said curtly, " I don't want to hear any confidential information; I am here in my official capacity. I have Sir Hercules Robinson in South Africa. I have entire confidence in him and I am quite convinced he will keep me informed of everything I ought to know."

It was a top-level snub, and one of the noble lords present had tactfully, but hurriedly, taken Dr. Harris out of the room. Shortly after this interview Chamberlain arranged the transfer of the Bechuanaland Border Police to the control of the Chartered Company, thereby demonstrating the uncanny perception of official ignorance, for the members of this handy little force served most usefully to swell the ranks of Jameson's invading army.

In Cape Town, the High Commissioner showed an equal aversion to official knowledge. Poor old Sir Hercules Robinson was over seventy and a little ailing. He had already retired once from the colonial service and for the last six years had been enjoying the not unprofitable calm of a directorship of the Standard Bank and also of Rhodes' own source of wealth, De Beers Consolidated. In February 1895 his successor in the High Commissionership, Sir Henry Loch—whose orthodox outlook Rhodes had found an unnecessary hindrance to his ambitions—resigned his office by a remarkable coincidence on the day following Rhodes' return from one of his visits to London, where these things were usually arranged. By an equally remarkable coincidence Sir Hercules, now armed with some pretty shrewd financial knowledge and influence, took up his old post again on the very same day, although he apparently suffered no particular economic need to take another job.

Rhodes told Sir Graham Bower, the Imperial Secretary in Cape Town, what was afoot in Bechuanaland and Bower said, "The old man ought to know." He took Rhodes into the High Commissioner's office and left them alone together. Later, Sir Hercules said to Bower, "The less you and I have to do with these damned conspiracies of Rhodes and Chamberlain the better. I know nothing about them." In the light of Chamberlain's own official reaction, the remark did the Colonial Secretary less than justice, although it confirmed his expressed faith that Sir Hercules would keep him informed of only those things he really wanted to know.

But Sir Hercules ordered Bower to allow the troops to come down from Bulawayo through Bechuanaland to Pitsani, and to arrange forage for them at the Imperial Post Office relay stations. It was a remarkably thoughtful

gesture on the part of someone who ostensibly knew
nothing about the "damned conspiracy".

Moreover, striving to know nothing about the whole
affair, the High Commissioner must have found it a shade
embarrassing to be told by Chamberlain that, in the event
of a rising, he would probably receive an urgent call to
proceed to Pretoria to act as mediator between the rebels
and Kruger's government. Chamberlain even indicated,
three weeks in advance, the date of the summons which was
to come so unexpectedly—the twenty-eighth of December,
a Saturday. At the time he was unguarded enough to write
to the hapless Sir Hercules, "I take it for granted no
movement will take place unless success is certain. A fiasco
would be most disastrous." Sir Hercules, in fact, was to
play the role of independent mediator in a dispute whose
outcome, in one particular direction, he was first to take steps
to insure. And the word "movement" was dangerously
allusive to Jameson's army, although neither the writer nor
the recipient was supposed to know anything about that.
Sir Hercules, with nostalgic thoughts of the restful calm of
Standard Bank board meetings, had good reason to damn
the conspiracies.

While the cabled messages passing between them might
have taken some explaining away, these high authorities
at least had the advantage of the use of an official cipher.
Rhodes and his fellow conspirators were not so fortunate—
or else the modern conception of security was not thought
necessary in those days—for the codes they resorted to were
so transparent as to be positively naïve. Even Moberley
Bell, the redoubtable editor of the London *Times*—whose
friendship with Rhodes promised him an exceptional scoop
—joined in the charade and wrote to his South African
correspondent, "I want to impress on Rhodes that we hope
the New Company will not commence business on a
Saturday, because of the Sunday papers." The *Times*, of
course, was not published on Sunday and, in Bell's view, it

would be inconsiderate, especially when arrangements were being made so far ahead, to fix the spontaneous rising for a Saturday.

Frank Rhodes, Cecil's brother in Johannesburg, was far more cryptic. He telegraphed Jameson, "Polo tournament postponed till after New Year so that it will not clash with Race Week." The second half of the message, of course, meant exactly what it said. However seething the discontent against the way of life in Johannesburg, it was inconceivable that the social round should be interfered with.

As December advanced, Jameson grew more impatient. There was such obvious lack of purpose in keeping his men unoccupied in the wilderness of Pitsani that he was at pains to prevent them packing up and going somewhere more congenial for Christmas. There was little to keep them in the deserted post station whose only architectural feature, advertised blatantly by swarms of flies, was the shed where the teams of mules for the mail coaches were kept.

Some of the men—probably those who had nowhere else to go—had been worked up to such a pitch with stories of the intolerable conditions in which their wretched fellow-countrymen lived in Johannesburg that they were all for breaking loose and riding valiantly to the rescue, arriving, if possible, in time for Race Week. Francis Newton, the Resident Commissioner at Mafeking, who heard all this on his frequent visits to the officers' mess at Pitsani, became justifiably disturbed. He felt it his duty to report to the High Commissioner at Cape Town and asked for an interview. But Sir Hercules was true to his trust. He said, "I won't see him. The whole thing is piracy. I know nothing about it."

Then, to Jameson's relief, Rhodes—whom history has so consistently vindicated of all foreknowledge of the raid—telegraphed on Monday, the twenty-third of December, that the rising would take place on the following Saturday at midnight. The convenience of the London *Times* was to be thoughtlessly disregarded. Rhodes instructed Jameson to start not earlier than eight o'clock on Saturday evening, and to destroy all telegraph communications along his march. He ended the telegram, "We suspect Transvaal is getting aware slightly," which was an unusual way of putting it. Then, remembering Jameson's besetting impatience, he must have regretted this last sentence and its implication of urgency, for next day he telegraphed, "You must not move before Saturday night."

As, in any event, Jameson did not move until after Saturday night, the generally accepted suggestion that he acted before Rhodes had any idea what he was about rings rather hollow.

But in Johannesburg the polo tournament, or company flotation, or whatever it was, had been postponed almost *sine die.* Jameson also had a brother in Johannesburg, Sam, and he cabled, "You must not move until you hear from us again." He added fraternally, "Too awful. Very sorry."

Jameson would have none of this. He had already sent out his men on the agreeable mission of cutting telephone wires, although the lines to Cape Town and Johannesburg were still intact. He replied ominously, "They have two days for flotation. If they do not, we will make our own flotation with the help of the letter which I will publish." The people of Johannesburg were to be saved whether they liked it or not, and if they objected Jameson was prepared to use blackmail.

Sam answered with brotherly frankness. He wired, "The public will not subscribe one penny towards it even with you as director. Ichabod." That was on Friday, the twenty-seventh, and the glory, even though it had been but potential, had verily departed.

The news of the anticlimax in Johannesburg had already reached London. On Sunday, the twenty-ninth, even Chamberlain had to acknowledge that it had come to his notice. He wrote to Lord Salisbury, the Prime Minister, "I think that the Transvaal business is going to fizzle out . . . and it is now quite possible that Kruger will make some concessions." He could make no mention of Jameson straining at the leash on the border because officially he knew nothing of it. But he had acute powers of perception, for on the same evening he cabled to the High Commissioner, "It has been suggested, although I do not think it probable, that an endeavour may be made to force matters at Johannesburg to a head by someone in the service of the Company advancing from the Bechuanaland Protectorate with police." The suggestion must have shocked poor old Sir Hercules, despite Chamberlain's specious doubts of its probability.

If the succession of telegrams from Johannesburg and Cape Town had confused the issue in Jameson's mind, the message delivered by Heany and Holden helped to clarify his decision. Heany arrived at Pitsani on the Sunday morning, the twenty-ninth, and Rhodes had instructed Jameson that he was not to move before eight o'clock the night before. Jameson had accepted Rhodes' instructions as part of the grand strategy—a detail of timing. If it were only a matter of waiting for the right moment in the development of the plan, he could be patient enough. But his brother's message—full of uncertainty—had kept him back during the night. To get some sense out of the confusion he had wired to Rhodes on Saturday, "Unless I hear to the contrary I shall leave to-morrow evening."

He received no reply to this, so on Sunday morning, after seeing Heany and hearing the message from Johannesburg enjoining him not to come, he sent a final telegram to Rhodes, "Shall leave for the Transvaal to-night." Then, lest there should be any danger of further telegraphic confusion, he cut the wire.

Although, to the chagrin of Moberley Bell, the war had been planned to break out during the week-end, the social round in Cape Town was apparently as insistent as in Johannesburg, for no arrangements had been made there to maintain communications between Rhodes at his headquarters and his general in the field. Jameson addressed his telegrams to Rhodes, "Charter", Cape Town, the telegraphic address of the Chartered Company. But although the telegraph office was open the Company's was not, and the two fateful little slips of paper, notifying that telegrams awaited collection, were pushed unceremoniously under the side door.

They were found by a conscientious clerk who, presumably with an eye to promotion, called at the office at eleven o'clock on the Sunday morning. He collected and read the telegrams and must have been impressed with their urgency for, regardless of expense to his employers, he took a cab to Three Anchor Bay, two miles from Cape Town, where Dr. Rutherfoord Harris, the Secretary, lived.

Dr. Harris, too, when he saw them, sensed that the messages were of some importance and might need replies, so he sent the clerk back to the telegraph office in a vain attempt to keep the line open to Mafeking. It was a point the clerk had overlooked. Not that he would have been in time to have had any effect for, being the sabbath, the Mafeking office had closed at half-past ten, and the worthy people of the little town had retired to their devotions and their Sunday rest, stolidly unaware that a few miles away, over the hills, an army was preparing to set forth on an invasion into a foreign land.

Dr. Harris, whose position had accustomed him more to this sort of thing, took the cab over from the clerk and drove the seven miles up the mountain road to Groot Schuur, shimmering in the sun under the towering crags of Devil's Peak. It was already afternoon before he handed to Rhodes Jameson's confirmation that he was determined to move that night. Not that Rhodes had probably ever expected him to do anything else. In any case, for once Rhodes showed little sign of urgency. There was at the house the usual Sunday company of the high lights of Cape Town society, and his only consideration seemed to be for his guests. The cab was prodigally kept waiting three hours before a reply to the telegram was ready and it was not until four o'clock that Harris returned to the wretched clerk still importuning a reluctant telegraph office to re-establish communication with the war. The clerk stayed at the office until seven o'clock in the evening before giving up the hopeless struggle, for Jameson had cut the wires anyway—which was poor reward for his enthusiasm of the morning. It was even worse reward to reflect that, had he stayed indolently at home, his superiors would have been saved a lot of fruitless exertions on the sabbath.

Late that night, assured in his own mind by then that Jameson could have received no message from him, Rhodes sent a servant on horseback to call Sir Graham Bower, the Imperial Secretary. He told him, " Jameson has taken the bit between his teeth and gone into the Transvaal." There was a general air of gloom and, on Rhodes' part, even distress, although the situation was the logical outcome of his own designs. It was too late at night to break the news to Sir Hercules and he was left in the bliss of his official ignorance of the whole affair until he arrived unsuspecting at his office at ten o'clock the next morning. His first reaction was, "Perhaps Chamberlain has sent him in or may approve his going. Chamberlain's such an extra-ordinary fellow he's capable of anything." Such was the measure of Sir Hercules' confidence in his chief.

When they heard the news in Johannesburg, the people Jameson had set out to save were as unappreciative as they were surprised. On the Thursday, the twenty-sixth, rumours had started circulating at the races. People had been talking of a rising for months, without any real belief in its serious intention. If they had believed in it they would have stopped talking about it. Now it was freely said on the course that Rhodes had fixed it for the week-end and that Jameson was waiting with an army on the border. Even so, it would have been difficult to find a committed rebel in Johannesburg outside the Rand Club.

On Monday, although nothing riotous had happened in the town on the fateful Saturday, the code game started again. A telegram from Cape Town said, "The veterinary surgeon has left for Johannesburg with some good horseflesh and backs himself for seven hundred." It was signed "Godolphin", which secret code was so successful that it was only discovered some years later that it had, in fact, emanated from Dr. Harris. The rest of the cypher was too cryptic even for the experts, until fortunately another message followed a few hours later from Mafeking, saying, "The contractor had started on the earthworks with seven hundred labourers and hopes to reach terminus on Wednesday." That was a more intelligible code, and in Johannesburg—in fact, all over the Transvaal—they knew Jameson was on the way. The people in Johannesburg, not unreasonably, were alarmed. It looked as if they would have to rise to protect the force that was coming to save them. That the message exaggerated the size of the force served little more purpose than to assure a stiffer resistance.

The Raid itself was an inglorious little episode and the least part of the story. The spirit in which Jameson undertook it was clear when he said, shortly before he set off, "Anyone could take the Transvaal with half a dozen revolvers." To an unattested general with a successful war against the Matabele behind him, this minor campaign against a bunch of farmers presented no problems. Perhaps that was why he never took the trouble to work out any plan.

Two forces started off—one, the army from Pitsani, and the other, a detachment of the Bechuanaland Border Police which Chamberlain had so conveniently transferred to the

Company's control. Stationed just outside Mafeking, it had been placed directly under Jameson's orders.

. An inspector of the Cape Police—Mafeking was, and is still, in the Cape—heard that the Border police were to fall in on the Sunday evening. It was a unique edict for a sabbath, and he sent a sub-inspector and a sergeant to find out what it was all about. The current story that this Sunday evening had been chosen to set off on an expedition against a native chief—who could be found at his kraal any day of the week—was a little improbable. Nor could the people of Mafeking seriously nourish the illusion that the men were off on a routine job when they heard the sound of cheering from the camp. It was unlikely there would have been any special enthusiasm for an assignment that served to diminish their Sunday leisure.

However, nobody thought it his duty to report what was going on—in fact, nobody would have been thanked by anyone for doing so. It was not until the sub-inspector and the sergeant returned many hours later, tired out from their long ride, and reporting that the force had actually invaded the sanctity of a foreign country, that the inspector felt it incumbent on him to notify his superiors in Kimberley. The telegraph wires were cut but, rather than rouse a man to repair them at that time of the night, he sent a horseman off on a fifty-mile ride to the nearest point of communication.

At Pitsani, Jameson had paraded his men in the afternoon. He read to them what he considered suitable extracts from the letter from Johannesburg which, incidentally, was now dated the twenty-eighth and had ostensibly arrived, by some miracle, at Pitsani overnight. The enthusiastic response to the letter's heartfelt cry was not all it might have been. Colonel Grey, at Mafeking, had wrung cheers from his troops much more readily without it. Jameson hurriedly substituted a more effective appeal with the promise of a special bonus. Generosity with the Company's money had always been one of his greatest attributes.

Before the parade—and now that the time for action had come—the officers, having their commissions to consider, expressed some doubt about the propriety of the whole idea. Sir John Willoughby, without the slightest authority whatsoever, assured them their commissions were quite safe and that orders—details of which were unspecified— emanated from the proper quarters. But his official report, made after the battle was over, reveals even in its introduction that he had no military authority behind him. He calls it the "Official report of the expedition that left the Protectorate at the urgent request of the leading citizens of Johannesburg with the object of standing by them and maintaining law and order whilst they were demanding justice from the Transvaal authorities. By Sir John Willoughby, Bart., Lieutenant-Colonel Commanding Dr. Jameson's forces." The oblique reference to the doctor is interesting. If Willoughby commanded, what was Jameson's position? The report covered action that took more explaining away than even the laudable intentions expressed in its introduction could achieve, and ultimately the whole affair cost Sir John his own commission.

The two columns met at five o'clock on Monday morning at Malmani, forty miles inside the Transvaal. In an impulsive moment of curiosity, to learn if their movement had been reported, they roused the sleeping telegraphist in the little town and asked if he had received and passed on any messages. In actual fact he had not, but when he saw an army of five hundred mounted men, eight maxims, three field guns, eleven mule-drawn carts, thirty pack horses and nearly a hundred native followers, all headed purposefully along the Johannesburg road, he quickly remedied the omission. Unfortunately, the men sent ahead by Jameson to cut the telegraph wires to Pretoria had taken with them a bottle of something sustaining and, in a flush of alcoholic enthusiasm, they had laboriously cut and buried two lengths of fencing wire, with little prejudice to the internal telegraphic communications of the Transvaal. By eight o'clock that morning the invasion was comfortably reported to the Commandant-General in Pretoria, and everybody along the line of march knew who and how many were coming. Old President Kruger had heard whispers of what was going to happen but, when pressed to take preventive steps, had said, " Wait until the time comes. Take a tortoise; if you want to kill it you must wait until it puts out its head, and then you cut it off." Now the messages were coming in that the tortoise was putting out his head. The security measures of the code about the contractor, in the telegram to be sent later that afternoon, became somewhat redundant.

On Monday evening, shortly before sundown, the army passed through a narrow defile in the Marico district where, sixty years before, the Boers had finally routed M'Zilikazi and sent the Matabele flying north. The senior officer of the district, Commandant Botha, let the tortoise put its head through the defile, but instead of cutting it off he delivered to Jameson a letter asking him, quite politely, to withdraw from the Transvaal Republic. It was an amazingly tolerant gesture on the part of a representative of a sovereign authority to a gang of unlawful foreign intruders, and it did infinite credit to those who sponsored it. Its patent offer to help him out of an awkward situation was quite lost on Jameson and he answered vaingloriously that he had come " in reply to an invitation from the principal residents of Johannesburg to assist in their demands for justice and the ordinary rights of every citizen of a civilized state ".

During his three days' march, Jameson received two more written requests to withdraw, and although these carried the additional weight of the authority to which he himself was answerable, he treated them with equivalent contempt. On Tuesday, a Sergeant White, who had ridden a hundred and sixty miles from Mafeking in fifty-two hours on one horse, caught him up with a message from Francis

Newton, and specific orders from the High Commissioner. Knowing Sir Hercules, and the way he had maintained his official aloofness from the plot as it had developed, Jameson chose to interpret the order as just another of the old man's attempts to cover himself, and disregarded it entirely.

But the High Commissioner was persistent in his old age. If he could not hold Jameson back by the coat-tails he was intent on standing in his path. On Wednesday, New Year's Day, Jameson was confronted by another order, this time from the British Agent in Pretoria. This faintly pricked, if it did not altogether penetrate, Jameson's conscience, for he replied, submissively for him, " Much as I should like to obey the order to retire, I have now no alternative but to go on, because the supplies in my rear are exhausted." But, lest he should seem to have been deflected from his unwavering purpose, he added, " and I am anxious to fulfil my promise to come to the aid of my countrymen in their extremity". He was growing tired of these messages—which had been pouring in for weeks now—that overlooked the dire straits of the people who kept sending them.

Jameson's army, which had conquered the Matabele so comfortably, met its Waterloo at Krugersdorp, a little town about twenty miles west of Johannesburg. The forced march from Pitsani had been a severe strain. In three days the army had come a hundred and fifty miles and for most of its journey small groups of Boers had hung about its flanks and closed in on its rear. By New Year's Day the men and horses were hungry and tired.

For some weeks Jameson's friends had been making arrangements along the route for forage and remounts, with remarkably ineffective attempts at secrecy. A suspiciously upstart company known as the Rand Produce and Trading Syndicate had opened trading stores along the road, ostensibly to buy maize for sale in Johannesburg and provide horses for the coach services. As there was no noticeable demand for horses and the Syndicate's stores seemed more interested in stocking bully beef and biscuits than maize, the concern had been looked on with a degree of mistrust for some time.   Not that it won any better repute from the men of Jameson's army.   The supplies were all too sparse for five hundred men and the horses proved to be of little use for their purpose, having apparently never been saddled before.

The doggedness of the Boers left the troops little time for sleep, and altogether, even had there been no opposition on the way, by the time they arrived in Johannesburg they would hardly have filled the role of timely liberators that had all along been Jameson's justification for his wanton act of aggression.

He had expected that at Krugersdorp there would have been waiting a posse of riders to welcome him effusively and escort him into Johannesburg.   In a revealing note to Frank Rhodes he had said, "I do not want to go in as a pirate."   Instead, before he reached Krugersdorp, there came to him two riders, not dashingly on horses, but furtively on bicycles.   One was an Afrikaner who, speaking the language, had been able to make the way for the two of them clandestinely through the Boer lines.   They brought Jameson two messages.   The first was a letter from Frank Rhodes saying, "The rumour of massacre in Johannesburg that started you to our relief is not true.   We are all right."   This was hardly what Jameson wanted to hear so, ever the hopeful buccaneer, he ignored its import and replied, "My men are in great heart, although a bit tired." This classic exchange of intelligence might have been lost to posterity, because Jameson tore up Frank Rhodes' letter. But someone later went to immense trouble and collected all the pieces from the veld.   The messenger hid Jameson's reply in the tube under the saddle of his bicycle which, as he was captured, he had to abandon.   Consequently the reply was never delivered, but, months afterwards, it was found by a mechanic in a cycle shop.

Less disturbing to Jameson than the news from Johannesburg was the second messenger's report that the Boers were preparing to resist his advance at Krugersdorp and that the only road along which he could take his guns and wagons passed through the town itself.

This was of small concern to the conqueror of Lobengula. But his second-in-command was not so sanguine. Willoughby, with a diffidence hardly worthy of the Blues, was all for avoiding a march through Krugersdorp " on the military grounds of the possibility of there being opposition in the town ".

Jameson, the amateur general, overruled him, and Willoughby, who must have wondered where he stood himself in the chain of command, yielded. However, before moving, he sent an imperious note to the Boer commander threatening that if his march were resisted he would shell the town. Jameson's foresight in bringing a proper army with field guns was to be vindicated. In his message, Willoughby added considerately that the women and children should be moved out of danger.

General Cronje, the commandant of the town, must have had little regard for human life, for he ignored the warning. In a matter of twenty-four hours he had gathered two hundred and fifty men from their farms in his own district of Ventersdorp—and that in the days before telephones—and had ridden ninety miles across country. Despite Jameson's superiority in numbers, and the alarming threat of bombardment, he calmly took up a defensive position three miles west of Krugersdorp.

At four o'clock in the afternoon of New Year's Day, 1896, Jameson's army came dispiritedly over the crest of a hill and looked down across a muddy valley. The road to Johannesburg ran straight across the valley and up the hill the other side. At the top of the hill were some mine dumps and buildings and behind their protection Cronje had disposed most of his men. Lower down the opposite slope was a farmhouse on one side of the road and some prospectors' trenches on the other. At the bottom, where the road splashed across a broad drift, was a corrugated iron hut and a stone kraal with high trees along its walls. Altogether, the features might have been placed expressly to provide cover for troops waiting to enfilade the road.

The guns were brought up and trained on the mine buildings at a range of about a mile, and shrapnel burst over the heads of the Boers as they lay safely behind their embrasures. There was no movement in the trenches or near the houses. Encouraged by the apparent weakness of opposition, Jameson's officers led their men down the slope and through the drift, and at the bottom the thin line of invaders spread out and prepared to charge uphill and drive the Boers from the opposite ridge.

In all the prodigal history of war there has probably seldom been initiated an attack that was at the same time so hopeless and so purposeless. A hundred young men, without even the inspiration of a compelling cause to atone their sacrifice, moved up the hill in face of a death so probable that it would have been inglorious. The Boers behind their cover opened fire and thirty of the hundred fell dead or wounded. Thirty more found what shelter they could on the almost featureless slope of the hill until the fatherly Boers came out to take them prisoner. One wounded man ungratefully shot dead a Boer who came to succour him. The others turned and ran. That is the story of the Battle of Krugersdorp and it was all over in a quarter of an hour.

After that, even Jameson had to acknowledge his inability to carry on dogmatically along the direct road to Johannesburg. He tried a detour across the veld and his army promptly lost itself. It had never been contemplated for a moment that the troops would have to leave the main road, so the staff had not felt constrained to provide itself with any maps. Local guides were enlisted and, considering they were asked to conduct a force of foreign invaders through their own country, the results were not altogether surprising. After a long and exhausting march the army found itself once more on the outskirts of Krugersdorp. The only comfort was that ñight was falling, which gave some protection from attack, although this did little to make up for the absence of any issue of rations during the last eighteen hours.

At daylight the next morning, January the second, Jameson moved his men to the south where the way appeared to be clear. But if he succeeded temporarily in evading the Boers, the shadow of old Sir Hercules was not so easily shaken off and yet another message from the High Commissioner, through the British Agent, found its way unerringly across what was to Jameson but trackless veld. This time it was to tell him that even their own government had issued a proclamation to all British citizens in the Transvaal calling on them " to abstain from giving the said Dr. Jameson any countenance or assistance in his armed violation of the territory of a friendly state ".

Jameson and his miserable band were to be outlawed. The fiction of official ignorance of his intentions was henceforth to be promoted to the status of authentic history.

As the army moved drearily on—the men had now been without anything to eat for twenty-four hours—the Boer horsemen, who knew every fold in the rolling Transvaal veld, set themselves purposefully for the final kill. Their methods were those they used every day in rounding up game and, even more appropriately in their view, vermin. Up wind and on each flank they harried their quarry, and down wind, across the face of a hill, they lay quietly in wait.

Once more Jameson, when he saw his way ahead barred at Doornkop, brought up his guns. But although the plan of campaign had envisaged the expenditure of considerable energy in dragging the guns more than a hundred and fifty miles, it had never contemplated that they would be

needed to take more than token action. It had assumed
that, once the guns spoke, resistance would crumble away,
so only a few rounds of ammunition had been brought
along and most of these had been shot away at Krugersdorp.
Not that they would have had any more marked effect on
the solid granite of Doornkop.

Now another factor appeared which had not been
anticipated in the planning. The foreign state, which had
been bombarded with high-explosive without any provocation, surprisingly replied with its own artillery. Although
Jameson's shelling had had no effect on the Boers behind
their defensive position, the Transvaal "Staats Artillerie",
with its six Krupp heavy pieces, had an unfair advantage
over the unprotected invaders and more young men were
killed. The first intelligent action of the whole campaign
occurred when one of the invaders ran up a white flag. If
he had only anticipated his flash of wisdom by twenty-
four hours, seventeen lives would not have been uselessly
thrown away, nor thirty-five young men grievously wounded.
Another thirty-five were never properly accounted for,
although it is safe to assume they made their way quietly
to Johannesburg and the race meeting. Whatever happened to them, their defection is significant comment on
the lack of worthy purpose in the army that had moved off
from Pitsani in a blaze of misplaced heroics.

It was Willoughby who negotiated their surrender to
General Cronje. One of the terms he accepted was to
undertake to pay any expense to which the Transvaal
Republic had been put in consequence of the raid—
another unproductive call on the unfortunate Chartered
Company shareholders. Magnanimously enough, although
some of his comrades opposed him, Cronje agreed to spare
the lives of the raiders.

The rest of the story has little to do with Rhodesia. That
link was broken when the force of Matabeleland Mounted
Police surrendered to the Boers somewhere in the middle

of the Transvaal. Jameson and his officers were carted off to Pretoria in farm wagons, like Girondists on the way to the Place de la Concorde—which was about the only revolutionary effect they accomplished.

The good citizens of Pretoria cried loudly for their execution. Their ultimate fate was less romantic. Shipped back to London, Jameson and Willoughby, and five of the other officers, were sentenced to terms of imprisonment which they served at Holloway—before it became London's prison for women—as " first-class misdemeanants ".

The whole captured force had been kept in Pretoria gaol but two weeks before they were handed over to the British authorities in Natal to be sent home. Jameson, and what were considered his thirteen most dangerous officers, were shipped in a troop-ship, the *Victoria*. Any demonstrative welcome when they arrived in London was forestalled by Scotland Yard, who sent its officers to arrest them at Gravesend docks, and they were taken the same afternoon to Bow Street police court by special omnibus.

For the other twenty-six officers, and four hundred other ranks, a special mail steamer, the *Harlech Castle*, was chartered—just one more item on the B.S.A. Company's bill.

The proceedings at the police court against Jameson and his colleagues came opportunely at the tail end of the London season, when Society was short of other amusement. On their appearance in the dock the prisoners were greeted with cheers, and the magistrate was at some pains to restore that dignity which Bow Street reserves for its more wonted clients.

Sympathy for Jameson and his colleagues had been generated by an unexpected agency. On hearing the first news of the Raid, the Londoners had felt some sympathy for the Boers whose country had been flagrantly violated for no apparent reason. It was a typically British reaction. Then the Kaiser had expressed in a telegram to Kruger exactly what the British were feeling themselves and, their reactions still being typically British, their sympathies swung the other way. Jameson, first denounced as a self-seeking filibuster, now became a national hero.

Jameson and his fellow officers were committed for " trial at bar "—one of those very English institutions based more on tradition than logic, but calculated to impress the watching world with the incomprehensible majesty of the English law. " Trial at bar " is conducted in the august Court of Queen's Bench by three judges, each of whom is entitled to deliver his own private judgment. It is a form of trial usually reserved for cases with treasonable ingredients. The charge with which the prisoners were arraigned was worded to sound as treasonable as possible, but the only law that could be stretched to apply to what they had actually done carried such mild sentences that in the Queen's Bench Division the arraignment inevitably produced an anticlimax.

They were charged that "within Her Majesty's dominions, and without licence of Her Majesty, they did unlawfully prepare and fit out a military expedition to proceed against the dominions of a certain friendly state—to wit, the South African Republic, contrary to the provisions of the Foreign Enlistment Act of 1870 ".

Jameson's counsel tried his best to prove that Pitsani Botluko was not within Her Majesty's dominions but, despite some telling exposures of the way that particular part of Bechuanaland had been bandied about between the Colonial Office, the B.S.A. Company, and even the Transvaal Republic itself, he was overruled. The involved legal arguments tended to dampen Society's interest and, by the time the six days' trial was over, Jameson and his friends had almost been forgotten by their supporters.

After sentence, they were taken to Wormwood Scrubs, where they were treated as common criminals, but the Home Secretary relented and they were moved to the less harsh atmosphere of Holloway. It was the end of a long journey from Pitsani.

When Rhodes heard the verdict and the sentence he said, "What a tribute to the rectitude of my countrymen who have jumped the whole world!"

The little doctor, whose unyielding spirit had repeatedly countered injury and fever on his epic journeys through Africa, gave up the will to live. Within four months it was recognized that if he remained in confinement he would die. He was released from prison solely for this reason and without any special consideration of who he was, and he lay desperately ill in a nursing home. The worst of his punishments was going on in his brain. He had ruined Rhodes, and Rhodes had never communicated with him since the day he left Pitsani.

But whatever Rhodes' faults, and however unscrupulous his treatment of men, his loyalty to Jameson was as unshakable as his ambition. After the Raid, he never repudiated Jameson by a single word. When the whole future of his cherished Chartered Company rested on the degree of his own complicity in the Raid, he never sought to save it by disowning Jameson.

But, being Rhodes, he kept his feelings to himself. He was too gruff in his own make-up to realize that Jameson would be waiting for a sign from him. Only once did he reveal his inner thoughts. He was in Rhodesia during the rebellion—a story we are coming to—when Jameson had recently been released from gaol. Someone came to Rhodes and, awkward and embarrassed, said he had bad news. Rhodes listened fearfully. He was told that Groot Schuur, his house in Cape Town, with all his personal treasures, had been burnt down. With obvious relief, and a smile, Rhodes said, "Is that all? I thought you were going to say Jameson is dead."

It was in January 1897, more than twelve months since he and Jameson had exchanged their last telegrams before the Raid, that Rhodes was in London to face a parliamentary enquiry. At the urgent insistence of Jameson's servant, who maintained the doctor was actually dying, Rhodes overcame the terrible shyness that had kept him away so long. He went to Jameson's room in the nursing home. The servant opened the door, and the two men whose names had been bandied together for a year across the very world, came face to face at last.

There was a silence, but before he closed the door, the servant heard Rhodes say gruffly, " Both of us have had a rough time, but you have had a rougher time than I."

As soon as Rhodes came to him the little doctor rallied. Rhodes had discarded the trappings of office almost contemptuously. He was human enough to have been bowed down for a short while. Great courage is not to be unflinching but, having flinched, to rally. Rhodes was always so convinced he himself was right that the censure of the whole world was quite incapable of deflecting him from his ambitions, mainly because he was that rare sort of statesman with ambitions, not for himself, but for an idea. Jameson, who thought he had brought Rhodes' world to an end, found that Rhodes was quite content with the one still left to conquer. So, he went back with him into battle and, when Rhodes died, took up his mantle. The mantle was a little oversize, but Jameson wore it nevertheless. Although Holloway Gaol had been the end of a long journey from Pitsani, the nursing home was to be the start of a far longer journey that took him to the Prime Ministership of the Cape Colony, the Presidency of the British South Africa Company, and a baronetcy; he survived Rhodes by twenty years, and to-day he lies close to the man he thought he had ruined, in that shrine in the Matopos which has been dedicated to " those who have deserved well of their country ".

The Jameson Raid was an interlude in the Rhodesian scene. In retrospect, its mock heroics can be placed where they belong. At the time it was not easy for the ordinary man in Britain to assess its values. The press of those days may not have been quite as blatant as it is to-day, but even then it was not above conditioning its readers to look on Jameson as a hero.

In the ranks of the ordinary man at least some sense of balance might have been expected. But the world of literature was hardly enriched by a poem, odiously entitled "Jameson's Ride", whose merits may be fairly judged from the last verse.

> "I suppose we were strong, were madmen,
>   Still I think at the Judgment Day,
> When God sifts the good from the bad men,
>   There'll be something more to say.
> We were wrong but we aren't half sorry,
>   And, as one of the baffled band,
> I would rather have had that foray,
>   Than the crushings of all the Rand."

This drivelling nonsense was from the pen of none less than the Poet Laureate, Alfred Austin, who had succeeded Tennyson in that distinguished office the year before. Perhaps, on second thoughts, its bathos is quite appropriate.

XIII

CHAMBERLAIN's predecessor at the Colonial Office had been a certain Lord Ripon. This versatile nobleman had held the office for a short spell in 1892, before the Matabele War, but thanks to the vagaries of the party political system, control of Britain's Imperial policy had passed to other hands the next year. In the happy manner of ministerial appointments, disregarding any special knowledge of the appointee's office, Lord Ripon, before taking on the Colonies, had been Viceroy of India and First Lord of the Admiralty. Despite such catholic experience in the brave old days of British imperialism, he held the sort of views which would have delighted the Labour Government that was to rule Britain half a century later.

Had control remained in his keeping in 1893, the Chartered Company could have expected even less support for their war than was rather grudgingly given them. But in 1894, Ripon's party was back in power, and himself in office, and he was at pains to make some amends to the Matabele for the way they had been treated by his opponents in the interregnum. To this end, he ordered that Jameson's harsh demand that the conquered savages should surrender their arms was to be construed "in a liberal spirit".

His edict propounded the first of many such courageous policies evolved by succeeding Colonial Secretaries in the comfortable security afforded by the protection of the Metropolitan Police. The white people in Matabeleland

172

obeyed because, in their trustful innocence, they had yet to learn that most British statesmen came to their decisions on colonial affairs without even an elementary knowledge of local conditions. So, at London's brave behest, thousands of rifles and tens of thousands of rounds of ammunition were left in the hands of a barbarous people simmering with resentment at their defeat.

Then, in 1895, with a gesture of artless liberalism that should have warmed Lord Ripon's generous heart, Jameson marched the police force out of the country.

Providence, not to be outdone, sent a scourge of rinderpest. The Chartered Company had already confiscated most of the Matabele cattle to meet its obligations of loot promised to the men who had fought and won its war. In theory they took only the cattle actually belonging to Lobengula and, if he had still been alive, he might have been surprised at the scale of his personal wealth. Most of what they left to the surviving Matabele the rinderpest killed. Then, to stamp out the scourge, they collected and shot the rest, and the Matabele had some difficulty in recognizing the advantages of the white men's occupation of their land.

In March 1896 there were fifteen hundred white people in Matabeleland. Of these, six hundred were women and children. Of the white population about half were in and around Bulawayo and the rest were spread thinly over the vast wilderness of the country. Lobengula's highly disciplined army had gone to war more than twenty thousand strong. Less than a fifth of these had been killed in the slaughters of Bembesi and the Shangani and, of the survivors who swarmed over the country now occupied by a handful of white men and women, over sixteen thousand were trained warriors brought up with battle in their hearts. They had suffered a shock at the hands of the white impis but were inclined to blame superior witchcraft. Then they heard of the ignominious defeat in the Transvaal of the men they had believed unconquerable and a more hopeful spirit prevailed.

The consequence was inevitable, and was much the same as the events which took place in Kenya more than half a century later. If, in any narrative of the Mau Mau rising, the name "Matabele" is substituted for "Kikuyu", the story could ring just as true of what happened over fifty years before. The only important difference is that the unpleasant treatment meted out by the natives to the white people of Kenya has not been one fraction of what the white settlers in Rhodesia experienced at the hands of the Matabele and Mashonas in 1896 and 1897. Where the Kikuyu have murdered in dozens, the Matabele massacred in hundreds.

Within a week of their rising they killed a hundred and thirty white men, women and children and, in the outside districts of Matabeleland, there was scarcely a white person left alive. The first attack, on the twenty-second of March 1896, in the Essexvale district twenty miles east of Bulawayo, accounted for seven white men, two native servants and an Indian cook. The same day another gang battered to death a family of eight—grandparents, parents and children. They used knobkerries and battle-axes and dragged their victims outside the house into the yard to give themselves room for their work. The local native commissioner was killed in his office. Two miners were murdered and their bodies mutilated. Later that evening a group of natives presented themselves to another mine manager for employment and, as a gesture of appreciation, turned and killed their new master. Altogether, it was a grim day.

Sixty miles away, in the Insiza district north of Bulawayo, there were two early attacks. One accounted for two doctors—one of whom had just brought his bride out from England. She first escaped into the bush but the natives found her and stoned her to death. Death at their hands was never very quick. The other attack disposed of two complete families who were spending a pleasant day together—two men, and nine women and children. Besides attacking unprotected families, the Matabele surrounded and fought it out with armed posts. A native commissioner, with a sub-inspector of police and four miners, held out for three days while their ammunition lasted, then they were beaten to death, in the contemporary manner, with knob-kerries. Before the first impetus of the rising had spent itself, a hundred and ninety white people had been killed in Matabeleland.

With their only organized defences squandered on a political adventure, the people of Bulawayo, who had their own families to look after, might have been expected to be able to offer little help to those isolated on mine and farm. But they gathered their women and children in a vulnerable laager in the market square—where the City Hall now stands in smug security—and organized rescue columns that soon boasted names as proud as any regiment of the line—Grey's Scouts, Napier's Scouts, the Afrikaner Corps. These men fought their way through to the lonely spots where little groups of white people were holding out, and fought their way back with them to Bulawayo.

At the time of the outbreak Rhodes was out of two jobs —no longer Prime Minister of the Cape nor Managing Director of the Chartered Company. By chance, he took a trip to Rhodesia in April, travelling again through Beira despite the Portuguese, who still held the port. This time there was no Jameson to meet him in Mashonaland and put a cheerful face on things when he drove into Salisbury through country littered with cattle killed by the rinder-pest. It had not been a very happy year since Jameson had seen it in with the Raid, and when Rhodes arrived in Salisbury the prevailing aura of gloom was hardly mitigated by the news that the Matabele had risen.

A relief column was being organized in Salisbury and,

when it left for the south in the middle of May, Rhodes accompanied it. The column was considerably stronger than anything the people of Bulawayo had been able to muster. It joined up with Grey's Scouts somewhere south of Gwelo and, working back towards Bulawayo, succeeded in routing a large impi of rebels at Umgusa Bridge, not far from the old site of Lobengula's kraal.

By June, the murderous outburst of the Matabele had spent itself. It had come disconcertingly near to complete success, despite its lack of coherent leadership. But when a relief force of real soldiers arrived from Mafeking, the rebels wisely withdrew into the Matopo hills. Another column of volunteers had come all the way from Natal, up the coast to Beira and into Rhodesia through Umtali. It was a long journey, and by the time they had passed through Salisbury they heard, not surprisingly, that all the excitement was over. But they were not to be entirely disappointed, for they found themselves at the vortex of another rebellion as bloodthirsty as they could hope for.

In June, the cowering Mashonas, whom the white men had held up to the Matabele as examples of how graciously to accept the new order, spread through their land the encouraging news that the Matabele had murdered all the able-bodied white men of Salisbury, who had gone to the rescue of their friends in Matabeleland. The opportunity of ridding themselves entirely of these people who insisted on making them work was too tempting and in a few days a hundred and nineteen people were murdered in the Charter district.

The story in Mashonaland was much the same as it had been in Matabeleland. An early attack on a farm at Hunyani Poort—just below the site of the dam that holds back Lake McIlwaine to-day—was typical. One morning, the labourers failed to turn out to work. The farmer and his three assistants left the house to investigate, and the missing Mashonas moved in and battered to death the farmer's wife, her infant daughter and a woman friend. The men were set on by another gang and murdered in the lands.

So often, human tragedies become epics. Material things —even lives—are lost, but the spirit of man shows a gain. The history of the Matabele and Mashona rebellions holds many such epics—many unrecorded, even unknown—and probably the most typical was the story of what came to be known as the Mazoe Patrol.

On the sixteenth of June, at the start of the Mashona outbreak, in the grand peace of the Mazoe Valley thirty miles north of Salisbury, hearing there was trouble in the district, the manager of the Alice Mine, with his young wife just out from England, called together his twelve neighbours, two of whom also had wives. He had no idea of the true scale of the rising, but had heard of what had happened round Bulawayo, and thought it wise for them all to move in to Salisbury.

They prepared for the journey and, on the morning of the eighteenth, set off calmly enough in a tented wagonette and a donkey cart. One of the men was down with fever and rode in the wagonette with the three women. Not a mile from the mine they were set on by Mashonas and two of the husbands were beaten to death. The party perforce turned back to the mine and, before they reached its shelter, another man was shot dead.

At the mine they made a makeshift laager, and Mr. Blakiston and Mr. Routledge, of the telegraph department, rode off on one horse to their office nearly a mile away. From the office they sent a message through to Salisbury. On their return ride to the laager they were both killed. If they had been killed on the way to the office, and no message had been sent, probably none of the party would have survived. The price of the message was high, but it was safely received, and the plight of the little outpost was known in Salisbury—no small tribute to the courage of the two men and to Rhodes' hobby of linking up Africa with his beloved telegraph.

There were many similar messages coming in to Salisbury that day, and the demand on police and volunteers was heavy, but an armed party of half a dozen men was spared and, in the evening, it set off to the mine, led by Lieutenant Dan Judson. He found the country teeming with berserk Mashonas and took nearly twenty hours to cover the thirty miles. What he had seen on the way convinced him that his force was too small to protect the party of unarmed civilians and see them through to Salisbury. He sent a Cape boy through the night with a request for at least forty men, but this was beyond the means of the authorities and they were only able to send twelve troopers under the command of Inspector Nesbitt of the Company's police.

It was more than forty-eight hours after the first attack before the party and escort—twenty-six men, three women and eighteen horses—moved off from the makeshift laager. They had armoured the wagonette by nailing sheet iron along its sides and back. The donkey cart was summarily abandoned. All the mules had been killed, so they in-spanned six riding horses in the wagonette, and the three women and the sick man—who was in poor shape—rode inside. Half a mile from the mine a lieutenant of the police was shot dead, then a horse, which had to be cut out of its traces under fire. It was not an encouraging start to a journey of thirty miles. As they struggled forward, two more men were killed and two badly wounded. The sick man gave up his place to the wounded and fought somehow with the others. The women, two of whom had seen their husbands killed before their eyes two days before, spent the time handing ammunition to the men and attending the wounded.

Through a long day, the little band fought every inch of the first twenty miles until they came out into open country. When, after nine miles of comparative safety, they came to Salisbury, there were only three horses left out of eighteen to drag the battle-scarred wagonette. Since the first attack, eight men's lives had been lost, but eleven of the original party from the mine were brought to safety. Inspector Nesbitt was awarded the Victoria Cross. That is the typical epic of the Mazoe Patrol.

In Matabeleland, another Victoria Cross had been awarded to Trooper Henderson who walked for three days through Matabele-infested country, supporting a wounded man on his horse.

When the rebels were at last defeated, the white men felt they really had the right to call the country their own. It was easy to forget they had come among the Matabele and Mashonas unasked, and not particularly graciously, and taken from them their land and their freedom. It was the fresher memory of native barbarity that left an indelible mark, and a legacy of antagonism and suspicion between the races that has never yet been properly erased.

XIV

IT was with a certain Colonel Carrington, then in command of the Bechuanaland Police, that Rhodes had first discussed in 1890 the prospects of occupying Mashonaland, and Carrington had given as his opinion that two thousand five hundred men would be needed to do the job, hinting that he would be happy to command them. Rhodes had turned down the suggestion, not too amiably, by saying he had no intention of embarking on an enterprise for the sake of making somebody a major-general.

By June in 1896, the Colonel had been promoted by the more usual method. At the same time, Rhodes, thanks to his friend Jameson, had been compelled to resign his directorship of the Chartered Company, and when he came to Bulawayo at the height of the unrest he no longer wielded his earlier undisputed control of affairs.

Major-General Sir Frederick Carrington was now in Bulawayo, whither he had been sent to quell the rebellion, and he at last enjoyed the consoling prospect of a long-drawn-out campaign. Expansive in his ideas as ever, he announced that this time he would need five thousand men to clear the rebels from the Matopo hills where most of them had gone to ground. He started pouring imperial troops into the operation—at the expense of the long-suffering Chartered Company—and, of the first thousand soldiers, he lost two hundred within a fortnight. Their effect on the Matabele hordes was negligible.

Rhodes was presumably as appalled by the wastage in

human life as by the expense to the Company. The military people were indulging themselves in just what he had been at pains to avoid at the time of the occupation. Johnson was no longer available to take the job on contract which, for the sake of his reputation, was probably just as well. But if Rhodes was incapable of understanding the military mind, there was one mind he understood better than any man in Africa, and that was the native's.

Rhodes began to talk of negotiating with the Matabele. Such talk sounded nonsense, almost treason, to a people who had been set on murderously by savages. Their instinctive inclination, being civilized, was to exterminate the savages—a solution which was to gain equally popular support when the Mau Mau rose sixty years later.

Whether it was Rhodes' sense of proportion or his sense of humanity that prompted him to pursue the alternative course must be left for students of the great man's character to decide. To exterminate tens of thousands of guerillas who have withdrawn into mountains and bush may be a more practical proposition to-day, thanks to the amenity of attack from the air, and the apparently bottomless purses from which military operations are paid for in our more enlightened times. In 1896, when the most lethal weapon was a burst of shrapnel—which tended to be singularly ineffective among the granite boulders of the Matopos—the operation was likely to involve expenditure in troops and money rather beyond the pockets of a handful of Rhodesian settlers.

From the humanity aspect, there was also something to be said for sparing the lives even of an uncivilized people. Less than ten years before, most of them had never known that such a curious species as the white man existed. Then he had suddenly intruded into their world and, by a superior form of witchcraft, had driven away their King, subjected them to servility, conscripted their young men to unaccustomed hard work, robbed them of most of their cattle, and shot the rest. They had known plagues before, and the remedy had been to exterminate the cause. They had set about exterminating the white men, and had very nearly succeeded.

Rhodes always looked on the natives as children and, although he was quite ready to take from them their land and their liberty, he still retained towards them a sense of responsibility. He ignored the understandable feelings of vindictive enmity harboured by those who had seen their friends and relations butchered by the Matabele, and he ignored too the natural inclination of the soldiers to look on primitive natives as an ideal enemy. He was unlikely to gain any support from General Carrington for a proposal to shorten the war, so he set off with his own friends in the general direction of the Matopos determined to treat with the Matabele, as he had always successfully treated with everyone else.

The land rises slightly to the south-east of Bulawayo and then falls away some hundreds of feet to an escarpment about ten miles wide, and along the middle of the escarpment the river Umzingwane cuts its course. It is a pleasant country down in the valley, more wooded and fertile than on the high veld round the town. Along the southern edge of the escarpment the Matopo Hills rise like a granite wall. From the northern side, the wall looks solid and continuous, but in reality it is broken by entrances to grassy valleys that wind and roll between, round and over, the lower slopes of the Matopos range. The range stretches for sixty miles and stands ten to twelve miles deep. It is a unique cluster of hills with its own grandeur and its own curious associations. It comprises no continuous mountain spur running in one particular direction, but a jumble of massive kopjes, some sheer and precipitous, some rounded and rolling, some rising to a thousand feet above their neighbouring valleys, and all littered with tremendous boulders—balanced in

comic positions by some supernatural practical joker—
which have been on the immediate point of crashing down
from their precarious perches for the last ten thousand
years.

It was into the fastnesses of these hills that the Matabele
hordes had withdrawn and been engulfed, and into which
Carrington's soldiers had tentatively penetrated to their
disadvantage. Viewed from the other side of the escarpment the hills looked virtually impenetrable, and even
Rhodes knew he would accomplish little by riding in
among them on the off-chance of meeting someone to deal
with.

One of the native commissioners found a likely emissary,
John Grootboom of the Tembu tribe from the Cape. To
him, and to the two companions he chose to take with him,
must go the undying credit for penetrating into the inner
councils of the Matabele when they had no idea what their
reception would be. In fact, recent events had indicated
that it was unlikely to be friendly. Grootboom was a
modest man, as all the finer African natives were, and still
are. After he had completed his mission he withdrew so
successfully into the background that the reward Rhodes
had promised him was never paid. His companions each
received a wagon and a span of oxen.

That Grootboom did make contact with the Matabele
chiefs which ultimately led to the rebels' surrender was
primarily thanks to careless feminine chatter. The three
emissaries were lying hidden near a path to a river when
two old crones passed that way to draw water, grumbling
about the hard times. They were clearly ripe to be
conditioned, as we say to-day. Grootboom must have been
something of a propagandist, for he presented himself to
the old ladies and persuaded them to go and nag their
chiefs until they agreed to come and meet him. He gave
them four days to wear down the obstinacy of their males.
He told them that if he heard nothing by then he would

go back to Rhodes, whom he hinted had some secret weapon that would blast all their people out of the Matopos.

On the fourth day, the feminine point of view prevailed. Even so, the chiefs were not taking any risks and ungallantly sent a very old woman to plant the prearranged signal at the place where they were to meet Grootboom while, from behind the safety of their rocks, they watched him for another twenty-four hours before they summoned up courage to come out and talk.

The few chiefs who had thus been contacted agreed to meet Rhodes if he came unarmed with only three others. It was less than sixty years before when Retief and his companions had been invited to meet Dingaan in very similar circumstances and the precedent established for behaviour at this sort of function can hardly have been encouraging. Yet it is to the everlasting credit of Rhodes and his companions that they never hesitated—in fact there was some unseemly competition for the honour of being included in the party. Rhodes took with him as his interpreter his old friend Johan Colenbrander, who had been his agent for a number of years in the old days at Lobengula's kraal, and who was equally respected by the Matabele themselves; a Mr. Vere Stent, who was a press correspondent attached to the imperial forces—the watching world was not to be forgotten; and, incongruously enough, Dr. Hans Sauer, who had been Jameson's adversary in the old controversy over smallpox—or perhaps pemphigus—in Kimberley.

The "first indaba", as the meeting came to be known, would have done credit to a modern conference of foreign ministers. The meeting agreed to arrange a meeting. At the next meeting, the "second indaba", which is the one that has become famous, Rhodes' party was to consist of himself and six others. The ban on arms still held, and there was, consequently, some consternation when Mrs. Colenbrander and her sister arrived at the camp the evening before Rhodes was due to set off, saying her native servant had warned her of a rumour among his people of intended treachery. When next morning, after sleeping on the problem, Rhodes and Colenbrander refused to be deterred by the rumour, the ladies matched their courage with the men and insisted on accompanying them to the meeting. Their presence at an occasion of this sort is probably without precedent in history.

The rest of the party of seven was made up by Armstrong, an assistant of Colenbrander; Jack Grimmer, Rhodes' secretary; and young McDonald, one of Rhodes' aides-de-camp who, as Sir James, was to write his biography and who, fifty years later—then one of the few remaining links with the great Rhodesian days of the nineties—was drowned through enemy action in the second World War.

Quietly, carrying nothing more lethal than riding whips, they rode to the appointed meeting place in the hills. The path wound between silent kopjes, fringed at their base with thick bush, ideal for ambushes. They came to a flat pasture land, circled by hills; on the one hand low kopjes behind which it was easy to imagine a regiment to be hiding; on the other the sheer face of a granite mountain.

In the centre of the open space some twenty unarmed chiefs waited beside a large ant heap which stood high out of the ground like an enormous boulder. The chiefs' appearance was already beginning to show that unfortunate influence which has ever marked the natives' contact with civilization. From the day the white men appeared, the Matabele abandoned their leopard skins and ostrich feathers and dressed themselves thereafter in discarded shirts, trousers, waistcoats and, whenever available, heavy overcoats to be worn throughout the hottest seasons. Here, in the Matopos, the chiefs had acquired some startling raiment, including military caps and uniform tunics of some of the smartest regiments of the British army; but somehow, what they gained in cover for their persons they lost in dignity.

As the party rode forward to meet the chiefs, the imagined regiment appeared with a flourish and pressed round the riders with a disconcerting realism—at least five hundred warriors with no false notions about dispensing with arms. Retief and his men must have stirred uneasily in their graves.

Colenbrander shouted, "Stick to your horses", but Rhodes never took kindly to other people's suggestions and he urged his horse through the Matabele ranks and jumped off and climbed up the ant heap.

He called loudly to the chiefs in their own language, demanding to know why they permitted their young warriors to disobey their own veto on arms. It was a typical Rhodes touch, forcing the chiefs immediately on to the defensive. To make even a pretence of authority they had to take Rhodes' part against the young warriors, and any solidity of front against the white man was immediately broken. The young men muttered and looked sullen, as natives reprimanded in a crowd mutter and look sullen to-day. At last one dropped his assegai, then another followed, and another, until the whole regiment stood unarmed, and a little resentful. In five short minutes Rhodes, unaided, had knocked the will to fight out of an army of vindictive savages. Before he had set off with his unarmed companions into the Matopo hills, the Matabele were still a sovereign fighting people needing a major-general and five thousand soldiers to defeat them; when he rode back to his camp but a few hours later, they had been transformed into a race of labourers and cook-boys for the white men. Paradoxically, it was the imperial troops who felt they had been cheated.

In actual fact the negotiations with the Matabele, in the accepted tradition of all negotiations with natives, took many weeks to complete, and it was a long time before the last of the chiefs came reluctantly out from their hiding places in the hills to acknowledge Rhodes as their master. He accomplished it all with an almost inhuman patience. It was a patience his own staff were seldom so fortunate as to experience. It even transcended the awkward breakdown in negotiations when one of the chiefs he was trying to placate reported that a party of British soldiers had broken into M'Zilikazi's tomb and looted some of the precious possessions that had been buried with the departed king for use on the other side.

It was when Rhodes went to visit the scene of this desecration that he took from the old warrior king the idea of being buried in the Matopos, facing north; and it was on one of the long rides through the hills during this time that he found the open-air cathedral at the top of a bare granite kopje which he called "The View of the World", and which he chose for his own burial place. There was dreadful consternation in his camp some time later when, in the maze of the Matopo kopjes, nobody could find his hill again. On that occasion, his whole staff was kept at the job of scouring the country for three days until, fortunately for their reason, McDonald found it; and Rhodes, M'Zilikazi's inspired successor, calmed down once more as he stood on the spot where one day his bones were to rest.

M'Zilikazi, the pagan savage, had come into the country brazenly, as an intending conqueror, making no secret of his purpose to take from the wretched tribes already living there, not only their land, but their cattle and women too. The white man, when he came with his boasted Christianity, pretended he wanted nothing but gold; but the ink was scarcely dry on the formal contract he had signed with Lobengula before he handed out promises to his own people, whom he was sending into the land, that when they got there it would be theirs. After a war and a rebellion, it was.

When Rhodes died, the white men gave him a Christian burial almost within sight of the heathen M'Zilikazi's tomb. And the simple Matabele who, for some strange reason, trusted Rhodes, gave his cortège their royal salute. Then, perforce, they put away the proud regimentals they had picked out for a funeral, and put on their new masters' torn shirts and shorts and went back to their work in the white men's kitchens.

XV

I F you had gone into the little round hut on a certain
April evening in 1947, fifty-four years after Lobengula's
camp had been burnt down, you would probably have
had first to push aside the ghosts jostling each other for
room on the horsehair couch, and then, in the darkness,
you might have been able to grope your way to the little
sashed window. Looking through, you would have seen
the back lawn of Government House festooned with fairy
lights and, discerning as ever, you would have guessed that
something unusual was afoot.

You would have seen the usually sombre square mass of
Government House itself bright with lighted windows. Up
the long avenue from Bulawayo comes a procession of car
headlights. Their steady beams give the avenue a dignity
it unfortunately lacks in daylight. It was one of Rhodes'
unfulfilled dreams that Government House Avenue,
stretching two straight miles from Bulawayo, should be
flanked by noble trees under which nursemaids would
wheel their charges in their prams. For a bachelor, Rhodes
showed a surprising grasp of family routine. Only the day
before his death he was badgering McDonald to "get that
avenue through. We have got to fulfil our promise to
give shade to the nursemaids in the afternoon." But
although there are trees along the road, they have little
ordered dignity, and the attempt at a noble avenue has
been a disappointing failure. The jacaranda-lined streets
in Bulawayo town are far better examples of what might
have been done.

The line of lights moves slowly up the avenue in unwonted discipline until each car, released at the gate after careful scrutiny, sweeps impatiently round the drive of Government House and disgorges its ladies on the big circular lawn before the front door. Then the cars move on, past the old indaba tree—with its own ghosts—close beside the drive, and the drivers park where Lobengula once stabled his wagon, and where his goats and sacred black cattle had been wont to graze. Khaki-clad successors of the pioneer police wave the cars to their places with urbane sophistication.

The goat dung and the flies have gone long since, but the grass and paths back to the house are still dusty and the men step gingerly in their shiny evening shoes. The ladies waiting on the lawn fuss with long white gloves and pretend to be accustomed to them.

With a solemnity befitting a papal conclave, the guests file slowly through the front door, across the hall and out into the central courtyard around which Government House is built. Through the centre of the courtyard runs a flagged path with soft grass on each side, fringed with gay flowers, and through the back wing of the house a porch with a grilled gate leads to the lawn with the coloured lights. As more guests arrive, the two lines grow, winding out along the lawn itself.

In the little hut, standing back behind tall trees at one side of the lawn, the ghosts crowd the sashed window, and some even peer round the buttress of the door, concerned to find out what is reducing their Rhodesian progeny to such unnaturally decorous behaviour.

It is a balmy April night and overhead the stars swing radiant and unwinking in the clear African sky. Suddenly, among the guests there is a hush and, here and there, a gasp of wonder.

Under the light shining over the door at the front of the courtyard stands a radiant woman in spreading white crinoline dress, with the bright blue sash of the Garter and, on her head, a sparkling tiara. Just behind her, standing almost shyly and self-effacingly, is a kindly grave-faced man. King George the Sixth of England, and his Queen, have come to Lobengula's kraal.

The King and Queen pass between the lines of guests, through the back porch to the lawn, and it is then that the ghosts inside the little hut start getting out of hand. They hustle straight through the mud wall of the hut and stand under the trees beside the lawn, crowding to the front of the lines of guests and staring unashamedly. Unfortunately, they fail to appreciate the identity of the lady in the shimmering white dress because, in their minds—which stopped registering new impressions sixty years ago—they see standing in her place a little old lady of tremendous dignity, with a crown perched on top of a lace cap hanging down over her shoulders. Hers is a proper crinoline, with evidence of thick iron hoops and countless layers underneath.

Little Doctor Jameson is standing in the front line of ghosts. When he sees the old woman, he says wistfully, " If only the old Chief were here to see her, too."

Someone moves behind him and, looking round, he can just make out in the darkness a great black ghost towering above him. A deep voice growls, " It is all right, Dakatele, I can see her. She is the Great White Queen." In the ghost's haunted eyes, admiration is struggling with fear.

At last the royal party walks back between the lines of guests, the King thoughtful and obviously tired, the Queen constantly stopping to speak to someone she recognizes— someone her memory has registered after meeting only once for a few short minutes. On the steps, beneath the light over the door, she pauses, and turns to leave with her Rhodesians a smile whose memory will not quickly be forgotten.

The royal family withdrawn, the guests troop out on to the lawn where tables are being set with food and drink.

Chief Umtasa breaks away from the spectral crowd under the trees and makes a bee-line for the whisky bottles. With tremendous dignity, befitting a foreigner who feels himself to be present on sufferance, Baron Rezende steps out to lay a restraining hand on the chief's shoulder, and Umtasa hisses a ghostly appeal for British protection. No one takes any notice. All the familiar faces are there—Selous, Gungunyana, Frank Johnson, Colquhoun and many others. Rhodes has found M'Zilikazi and they are comparing impressions of Matopo dawns and sunsets.

Only Lobengula stands by himself, watching the white men and women laughing and chattering before him. "Where," he cries mutely, "where, oh where, are my people?" The leaves in the trees above him rustle an echoing sigh, and a woman on the lawn shivers and draws her wrap around her bare shoulders.

At last the band on the terrace strikes up "God Save the King". The ghosts stare ahead, the anthem conjuring up for each one his own indelible memory of sixty and more years ago; the guests, thinking of the beloved family going to their beds close beside them under the old thatched roof, sing more fervently and with more meaning than ever before. Then, quiet and reverent again, they stream back through the courtyard and across the hall, out past the indaba tree to their motor cars.

Across the lawn beneath the fairy lights, to mount supernal guard over the King and Queen of England, ride Allan Wilson and his Shangani Patrol. The ghosts, black and white, all acknowledging them Brave Men, stand in mute salute under the rustling trees and watch them pass.

Then, one by one, the ghosts themselves move silently away; some to their enduring memories in the little round hut; others—M'Zilikazi, Gungunyana, Lobengula, even tipsy old Umtasa—to their Valhalla under the indaba tree, where they reflect, without much consolation, that they lost a kingdom and gained a flag.